HEROES OF GOD SERIES

HEROES OF GOD SERIES

This is a book in the HEROES OF GOD series.

Other books in the series include:

PAUL, THE WORLD'S FIRST MISSIONARY
  by Albert N. Williams

JEREMIAH, PROPHET OF DISASTER
  by Virginia Greene Millikin

QUEEN ESTHER, STAR IN JUDEA'S CROWN
  by Laura Long

DAVID, WARRIOR OF GOD
  by Juanita Jones

SIMON PETER, FISHER OF MEN
  by Albert N. Williams

The series will include books about John the Baptist, Luke, Joshua, Joseph, Elijah, Tyndale, Francis of Assisi, Martin Luther, and other biblical, historical, and modern church pioneers of our religious heritage.

The HEROES OF GOD series is under the general editorship of Albert N. Williams and Ann West Williams.

NARCISSA AND MARCUS WHITMAN
MARTYRS ON THE OREGON TRAIL

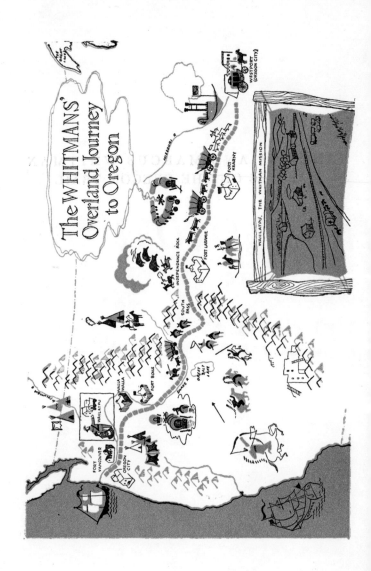

Narcissa & Marcus Whitman

MARTYRS ON
THE OREGON TRAIL

The story of the first American missionaries
to make the covered wagon crossing

by

ANN WEST WILLIAMS

ASSOCIATION PRESS
NEW YORK

The author is indebted to the Oregon
Historical Society for permission to quote
from the Letters and Journal of Narcissa
Prentiss Whitman, published in the *Trans-
actions* of the Oregon Pioneer Association
of 1891 and 1893, Portland, Oregon.

 55

Printed in the United States of America
American Book–Stratford Press, Inc., New York

For my Mother
Cora Smith West

CONTENTS

9

1. THE WEDDING

IT WAS A COLD FEBRUARY MORNING in the year 1836. In the little Congregational church in the village of Angelica, New York, a tall, blond young woman stood proudly beside a stocky, determined-looking young man. They had just been married. Miss Narcissa Prentiss had in that moment become Mrs. Doctor Marcus Whitman.

Near at hand Narcissa's mother and her sisters wept quietly into their tiny linen handkerchiefs, and her father, Judge Stephen Prentiss, looked sternly and blindly before him. The mother's tears and the father's grim face were not caused merely by the marriage of a dear daughter. Her parents were sensible folk, and they had long known that someday she would marry and leave them to make a home of her own. But they had always thought that her home would be on the next street, or, perhaps, in the next village. They had not counted on Dr. Marcus Whitman. The home which he planned to establish for his young bride, Narcissa, was not to be even in the same state, or in the same country.

He was taking her to the Northwest—to the far-off territory of Oregon.

Marcus Whitman was a missionary. In marrying him, Narcissa had willingly accepted the great task of carrying the message of Christ to the strange and distant land of Oregon, three thousand miles away from her home and family, from her church, from her friends, and from her pleasant and comfortable teaching job at Miss Willard's fashionable school for girls.

As a young girl, she had dreamed of being a great opera singer, for she had a lovely voice. But it was not to the concert halls of Paris and London and New York City that she was to turn her steps, but across the great empty western deserts and mountains where no white woman had ever before traveled.

Indeed, she had been told that no white woman, and particularly no white woman who had been reared as gently and carefully as she had been, could even endure the terrible hardships and dangers which lay on the Oregon trail. She was planning to undertake the impossible.

The silence of her thoughts was broken by the hymn which Narcissa herself had requested:

> *Yes, my native land, I love thee,*
> *All thy scenes I love them well,*
> *Friends, connections, happy country,*
> *Now, I bid you all farewell.*

It was the missionary hymn that was always sung to speed God's travelers on their ways. One by one the voices of the wedding party fell silent, until at last only Narcissa's clear, unwavering soprano could be heard.

2. THE FOUR WISE MEN
FROM THE WEST

FOUR YEARS EARLIER—in the spring of 1832—four Indians of the Flathead tribe had come to the city of St. Louis from the distant Oregon territory. That land, which was then so strange to Americans, is now covered by the states of Washington, Oregon, and part of Idaho.

Oregon was not at that time owned by the United States. According to a treaty which had been signed in 1818 and renewed in 1827 by the United States and Great Britain, both of whom had strong claims to the region, it was held by both of them in what was called "joint occupancy." This meant that both countries had the right to explore and settle, and to establish fur companies, until a final agreement could be reached. Actually, in 1832 and for many years later, Great Britain was the only country which took much interest in the territory, for the British-owned

Hudson's Bay Company, the great fur monopoly, was in almost complete control of the entire Pacific Northwest.

When the visiting Indians were taken to see General William Clark, Superintendent of Indian Affairs in St. Louis, they told him that their people had heard of the white man's Book and of his God from the officials of the Hudson's Bay Company and from the fur trappers who wandered into their lands. They had been told that the reason the white man was so strong and so powerful was that he read from the Book and worshiped the God of that Book, and they were eager to learn the white man's mighty religion. The four of them had come as messengers from their tribes to ask that white teachers be sent into the distant western Indian country to teach them the Book.

But General Clark, busy with more urgent problems, paid little attention to their requests, and at last, after two of them had died from sickness they had contracted during the course of their long journey, the other two prepared sorrowfully to return to their own far country. One of them made a last appeal to the General: "I came to you over a trail of many moons from the setting sun. . . . I came with one eye partly opened, to bring more light for my people who sit in darkness. I go back with both eyes

closed. How can I go back blind to my blind people?
. . . My people sent me to get the white man's Book
of Heaven. I am going back the long sad trail to
my people of the dark land, and I go without your
Book. . . . You make my feet heavy with burdens of
gifts . . . but the Book is not among them. When I
tell my poor blind people . . . that I did not bring the
Book, no word will be spoken by our old men or by
our young braves. One by one they will rise up and
go out in silence. My people will die in darkness,
and they will go on the long path to the other hunting grounds. No white man will go with them and
no white man's Book will make the way plain."

Although General Clark was not moved to action
by these stirring words, the appeal was copied down
by an Indian agent and sent to the *Methodist Christian Advocate,* a church newspaper, which published
it on March 1, 1833. The indignation and the pity of
Christian people in the East, who had thought little
of far-distant Oregon, were aroused by the desperate
cry for help from the "Four Wise Men of the West,"
as these Indians came to be called.

The Christian people did not express their deep
concern merely in words. They also dug deep into
their pockets.

Money poured into the coffers of the American
Board of Commissioners for Foreign Missions, which

represented the Presbyterian and Congregational Churches. Only the lack of money had hitherto prevented this Board's establishment of a mission among the Oregon Indians, and now, at last, they were able to give reality to a plan of long standing. A missionary could be sent.

Dr. Samuel J. Parker, a Presbyterian minister, was chosen to be the Board's pioneer missionary to the Oregon territory, and he set out immediately on his long journey. Unfortunately, he arrived in St. Louis too late to join the fur caravan of 1834, and he did not dare to travel into the unknown country without guidance and protection. Back to the East he returned, to tell the story of Oregon and to enlist helpers in the great task which he proposed to attempt again the following year. Among those to whom he talked were Dr. Marcus Whitman and Miss Narcissa Prentiss.

As a young boy Marcus Whitman had wanted to become a minister, but his family had opposed his choice because they were too poor to pay for the long college training which was required. In those days the profession of medicine did not involve so long and arduous an education as it does today, and Marcus' family persuaded him to become a doctor instead of a minister.

But Marcus did not forsake his dream, and long

before the appeal of the "Four Wise Men of the West," he had offered his services as a medical missionary to the American Board of Commissioners for Foreign Missions. The Board had turned down this first application because his health was poor, but now his strength had improved enough that he was readily accepted as a companion to Dr. Parker for the trip westward to be made in the spring of 1835. The two emissaries were instructed to report on the chances of success which a Christian mission might expect in Oregon.

But before leaving on his journey, Whitman was sent by the Board to talk to Narcissa Prentiss, who had dismayed her friends and scandalized her relatives by offering herself as a missionary to the western Indians.

"Why do you want to do such a thing?" her sisters had asked her. "If you want to go into church work, there is so much to do here."

"It is what I must do," she replied calmly. "I know it in my heart, and I feel that it is what God means for me to do. There are many here to work in the church, but there are few to teach the Indians."

When Marcus Whitman called on Miss Prentiss, he intended to point out that it would be almost impossible for a young unmarried woman to be accepted by the Board as a missionary. There were too many dangers, and she would have no protector. But his serious lecture was soon forgotten as he looked into her steady blue eyes and listened to her calm, courageous voice telling him why she had decided on such a difficult work. As he talked to her, he knew that at last he had found the woman whom he wanted for his wife.

At first Narcissa took Marcus for a rather ordinary young man, with no family and little education. But his eyes flashed and his shyness was forgotten as he spoke of the great service which lay ahead of him. She forgot his commonplace appearance, his prematurely graying hair, and his stooped shoulders, and when he asked her to marry him, she accepted without a moment's hesitation. There was no time for the pretty speeches and blushes of a courtship, but both of them knew that they had made no mistake in their hasty engagement.

It was a strange match in the eyes of the world. A daughter of the important Judge Prentiss had accepted a nobody for a husband. It was true enough, the town ladies murmured behind closed doors, that Dr. Whitman's family went back to the seventeenth century in New England, but it was not an influential family. His father had been nothing more than a village tanner and innkeeper. But, they concluded, raising their eyebrows and pursing their lips, Narcissa had always been rather a headstrong girl, even if she was a dutiful daughter. She would see to it that she got her way. Take this business of going to Oregon as a *missionary*, of all things! She would soon find out that she had thrown away her life.

But such criticism and gossip, when she heard it, bothered Narcissa not at all. She simply smiled and returned to her sewing, for there would be many things which a new bride would need, even if she was going to spend her wedding trip on the desert.

So, when Marcus went westward with Dr. Samuel Parker in the spring of 1835, he went with Narcissa's promise that on his next trip she would be with him as his wife.

On this first journey Marcus went only as far as the Green River in Wyoming, to the rendezvous where the fur companies and the Indians held their great annual meeting for barter, business, and pleasure. The information which he and Dr. Parker received there gave them great encouragement, and they decided that Dr. Parker was to go on to Oregon and prepare the way, alone. He was to pick mission sites and make friendly arrangements with the Hudson's Bay Company and with the Indians, while Marcus was to return east immediately to organize a caravan for the following spring.

The trips to Oregon had to start in the spring of the year. It was impossible to travel in the Rocky Mountains during the winter because of the terrible snows and blizzards, and therefore every pioneer party had only the spring and summer months in which to make the long westward crossing.

Back to the East Marcus hurried, impatient to claim Narcissa for his wife and with her to undertake their great adventure. With him he took two Indian boys, Richard Tackitooitis and John Ais, who were to go to school to learn about the white man's God, so that they could help to teach their people.

And so in February, 1836, Narcissa Prentiss married Marcus Whitman in the little church of Angelica, New York, and pledged her life to carrying the Word of God into the dark lives of the far-western Indians. She knew that danger and hardship and privation lay before her, but in her courageous heart there was only gratitude that she had been found acceptable for the great work which awaited her and her husband.

3. BUFFALO STAMPEDE!

IT WAS NOT AN EASY MATTER to arrange for companions for Marcus and Narcissa Whitman on the Oregon trip. Many who had come forward with quick enthusiasm in response to the "Four Wise Men" found many excuses when their first excitement began to wear off, but at last a group was organized. The Reverend Henry Spalding, whom Narcissa had gone to school with and knew well, and his wife Eliza were to go with Marcus and Narcissa as missionaries, and William H. Gray was to go as a mechanic and farmer to help establish the mission. Craftsmen like Mr. Gray were as badly needed in a new country as ministers and teachers, for their skills were invaluable in carving settlements from the untamed wilderness.

The two Indian boys, Richard and John, were returning to their own tribe, and they would be able to help a great deal with the cattle and horses which the missionaries planned to buy.

Early in March Narcissa Whitman set forth upon her honeymoon, surely one of the strangest and most stirring in all history. During the long trek across the plains and the mountains she kept a journal and wrote long letters to her family. She was not to get an answer to many of these letters for several years, for most mail from the East to Oregon was sent by ship around Cape Horn, then to the Hawaiian Islands, then to San Francisco, and at last up to the Columbia River and to the mission. The journal and the letters, written with great observation and lively curiosity, are filled with details of a journey across the continent in those days before the railroad and the airplane, even before the rutted wagon roads of later emigrations.

The hardships of this journey, as Narcissa described them in her journal, were not raids by yelling Indians, flourishing tomahawks and shooting flaming arrows. They were not the crossings of great rivers, swollen by melting snow and heavy rains. They were not starvation or thirst.

Fear of the Indians was to come later, when the tribes felt themselves threatened by the great numbers of white men crowding into the West. The wide rivers were bypassed on the trails picked by the

American Fur Company, with which the Whitman party traveled to the Rocky Mountains. There was no real starvation, for when fresh food ran out, there was always dried buffalo meat, called "jerky." There was no great danger of thirst, for the many water holes and springs of the western plains and mountains had not yet been polluted and destroyed. In later years the covers of long grass which protected the water holes were ruined by the thousands of thirsty cattle which trampled them, and emigrant companies were to find nothing but dry gullies where fresh, sweet water had been.

No, the hardships which faced Narcissa on this journey were ordinary things, the drudgery and monotony of her daily life. There was the driving necessity for continual movement, for the mountains had to be crossed before the snow fell. There were the crossings of tiny streams with sharp, twenty-foot banks. There were the tensions which grew up among people thrown together for months on end with no chance for privacy. There were weeks with no bread, no fresh vegetables, no wood with which to build a fire. Hardships like these, as commonplace as they seem, broke the spirits and ruined the health of many a sturdy traveler, but the gently bred Narcissa bore them all with courage and an unfailing sense of humor.

The first stage of their journey was by sleigh through snow and mud to Hollidaysburg, Pennsylvania, where they took passage on the Pennsylvania Canal to Pittsburgh. From there to St. Louis they traveled by steamer down the Ohio River, joining company with Henry and Eliza Spalding at Cincinnati. In St. Louis, Marcus made arrangements with the American Fur Company to go by boat up the Missouri River as far as possible and there to join the company's annual caravan to the rendezvous. Henry Spalding was sent ahead by land to await them at Council Bluffs with the two wagons, the cattle, the horses, and the mules, which the two Indian boys sneered at as being no good to chase buffalo.

Marcus, with Narcissa and Eliza Spalding, waited at Liberty Landing, many miles up the river from St. Louis, for the fur company boat. But the boat passed by deliberately, perhaps to indicate the hunters' disapproval of so wild a project as taking two white women across the prairies.

Narcissa's honeymoon, which had been a fairly leisurely and comfortable one to this point, now became a mad rush against time. The missionaries *had* to catch up with the fur company. Without that protection they knew that they would not dare to go forward through unknown and perhaps treacherous country. Recalling Henry Spalding from Council Bluffs with the horses and wagons, Marcus reorganized the party for the desperate trip. Without the two Indian boys the missionaries would not have succeeded, for there were several difficult streams to cross with the cattle and wagons. At the Elkhorn River crossing, Narcissa wrote to her friends in the East, "They [the Indian boys] came up to the river before us, and seeing a skin canoe on the opposite side, they stripped themselves, wound their shirts around their heads, and swam over and back again with the canoe by the time we came up. We stretched a rope across the river and pulled the goods over in the canoe without much difficulty."

On the last day before reaching the Loup Fork of the Platte River, beyond which it was dangerous to travel without protection and where they hoped to overtake the fur company, the little band attempted to keep going without a stop until they reached their destination. ". . . a part of us succeeded," Narcissa wrote. "Those in the wagon drove there by 11 o'clock, but it was too much for the cattle. There was no water or feed short of this. We rode with Richard and John until 9 o'clock, and were all very much fatigued. Richard proposed to us to go on and he and John would stay on the prairie with the cattle, and drive them in the morning. We did not like to leave them, and so we concluded to stay. Husband had a cup tied to his saddle, in which he milked what we wanted to drink; this was our supper. Our saddle blankets, with our Indian rubber cloaks, were our beds."

They reached the Loup Fork the next morning and found, to their deep gratitude and relief, that the fur company was still encamped there. By noon they were on the move again, knowing that they must remain with the caravan at all costs.

To Narcissa's marveling eyes, the caravan was a moving town. Each morning, long before daybreak, she was awakened by the cry "Arise, arise." She rushed to dress, to make breakfast, and to help Marcus break their camp and put out their campfire. Around her, dozens of other campfires were destroyed as the fur hunters and trappers finished their quick breakfasts and mounted their horses. By six o'clock she was on the trail again, hurried by the shout "Catch up, catch up!" Many a morning, as she sleepily mounted her horse or climbed into the wagon, she longed for one of the good down pillows of home and a chance to sleep until noon.

The long line of wagons quickly formed into traveling order. The caravan, headed by Captain Thomas Fitzpatrick of the American Fur Company, followed by the pack mules, the wagons, and the little group of missionaries, started once more to cover the daily allotment of twelve miles.

At eleven, Narcissa, half-asleep from the sun and the dust, slipped down from her horse as camp was made for a few hours' rest in the hottest part of the day. But her lunch table was not made of fine polished wood, and it was not spread with white linens and silver and sparkling china. "Our table is the ground, our tablecloth is an India rubber cloth, used when it rains as a cloak," she wrote. "Our dishes are tin basins for tea cups, iron spoons and plates for each of us, and several pans for milk and to put our meat in when we wish to set it on the table. Each one carries his own knife in his scabbard, and it is always ready for use. When the table things are spread, after making our own forks of sticks, and helping ourselves to chairs, we gather around the table. . . . It is the fashion of all this country to imitate the Turks. . . . We take a blanket and lay it down by the table, and those whose joints will let them follow the fashion; others take out some of the baggage."

Once again at two, refreshed by her brief rest, Narcissa mounted her horse. The caravan went forward over the rough country until six o'clock, when camp was made for the night. Once more, the great protective circle of tents and wagons and carts was

formed. Inside the enclosure all of the animals, except the cows, were loosed. The cows were tethered
outside to graze, and guards were posted for the
night, for this was country where the Indians were
none too friendly. They would steal anything that
wasn't tied down and guarded, Captain Fitzpatrick
warned Narcissa.

Narcissa and Marcus, thankful that another day of
weary traveling was over, pitched their tent, cone-
shaped and made of bedticking, large enough for
all of their party to sleep under. Their bedding was
the same India rubber cloth which they used as a
tablecloth, covered with blankets.

As the great sky of the western plains darkened to
deep blue, light from the campfires flickered on the
tired faces of the missionaries. Soon after nightfall,
while the members of the fur company still sat about
their suppers, Narcissa said her prayers and sank
wearily upon her blankets. The ground felt as soft to
her as the feather beds of home, and in a moment
she was asleep.

In this fashion, the caravan moved slowly and
steadily across the plains.

As the long weeks passed, Narcissa watched her
food supplies gradually dwindle away. The last of
the bacon was fried; there was no more flour for
bread and biscuits. But just as Narcissa was begin-

ning to wonder what she could give her husband for supper, the caravan entered buffalo country, and the hunters of the fur company and the two Indian boys brought in fresh meat. Narcissa liked it at first, but when the juicy fresh meat was replaced by the dry and nearly tasteless buffalo jerky, she longed for even a stale crust of bread and wrote home to her sisters that they must never waste even the driest piece. The little flour that she had left she used for thickening the buffalo broth soup.

This limited diet agreed with Narcissa, with all of them, in fact, except Eliza Spalding, who became so sick that for a time it was feared she might even die on the trail, as so many white women were to do after her. She begged her husband to go on and leave her, but at the rendezvous there was fresh food and she soon grew stronger. Her courage, like Narcissa's, never failed.

If it were not for the wagons, Narcissa often thought to herself, she could really enjoy the journey. Food and fuel were no problem at all compared to their troubles with those great lumbering vehicles. But Marcus was right, of course. He had often told her that unless wheels could cross the prairies and the mountains, settlers would never make the Oregon trip in any numbers. Until emigrants could take their wives and children and enough supplies for the trip, they would refuse to leave civilized country, and he was determined to prove that wagons could go through.

Day after day, Marcus stubbornly forced the wagons on toward the west. It was a good day indeed when the men of the party were not drenched and nearly drowned while trying to take the wagons across rivers, or when they did not struggle time and time again to right the wagons which upset in the rough country.

Many of the things which the missionary party had brought with them were abandoned to lighten the load. Clothing, bedding, everything that was not absolutely necessary was left to rot in the rain and sun, but even this desperate step did not make the task easier.

At Fort Laramie, Marcus decided to make his unequal battle with the wagons a bit fairer by leaving the heavy farm wagon behind, but he persuaded the fur company, which had always left their carts at the fort and packed mules on to the rendezvous, to try to take one of their carts forward.

From Fort Laramie in Wyoming, the weary trek continued. Narcissa sat in the lone light wagon and nursed the sick Eliza Spalding as well as she could, or rode sidesaddle on the tall horse which had carried her safely across many swift rivers.

As they approached Independence Rock one morning late in May, Narcissa, who had been riding quietly along in the jolting wagon, hearing faintly the usual noises of the cattle and the shouts of the men, and dreaming of home, was startled by the sound of shots and loud shouting from the head of the caravan.

"What is it, Marcus?" she called out sharply.

Her husband spurred his horse to ride ahead, but at that moment one of the hunters of the fur company galloped toward them. "Close ranks!" he shouted. "Buffalo stampede!"

Every man that could be spared from the frightened and milling cattle and pack animals rushed forward as the scattered caravan slowly drew together. The burst of shots from ahead grew heavier.

Through the cloud of dust Narcissa, frightened but trying to quiet the sick Eliza, could see the great herd of buffalo, which had been hidden by the hills and which was now pouring down upon the caravan without warning. On it came, straight for the defenseless train, until the desperately firing men found themselves threatened by stampeding animals. The horses and the mules plunged and reared in panic. Suddenly, at the last moment, as Narcissa offered a silent prayer, the leader of the herd turned, and the hundreds of huge buffalo rushed alongside her wagon. The earth trembled with the thunder of their hooves.

The caravan had been saved from almost certain destruction.

4. THE RENDEZVOUS

ON THE EVENING of July 6, 1836, the caravan, accompanied by a few Nez Percé Indians who had ridden out from their camp to welcome the missionaries, reached the annual fur company rendezvous on the Green River, a northern branch of the mighty Colorado.

As they rode into the huge sprawling encampment, Marcus Whitman watched his wife's face with amused delight. This was no new scene to him, for he had been to the rendezvous the year before, but to Narcissa it was as strange as if a story from the *Arabian Nights* had come to life.

As she alighted from her horse, the Indian women rushed forward and greeted her with hearty kisses. The Indian men gravely and curiously watched her, and the little children hung back shyly and stared. She was indeed a curiosity, for she was the first white

35

woman most of them had ever seen—and a white woman with golden hair.

The rough mountain men—remembering manners they had almost forgotten—took off their hats and greeted her respectfully. To her husband they spoke harshly, for they felt that this was no country for a well-bred American woman, no matter how courageous she might be. They even spoke of complaining to the government authorities in the East and forcing Narcissa and Eliza to return.

But Narcissa laughed and joked about the hardships of the trip until they laughed with her in open admiration.

The rendezvous was a regular summer event. In these great empty spaces of the West, where a man could live and hunt for years without seeing another human face, the rendezvous was the market place.

Here the Indians and the fur company trappers and the independent trappers who worked for no man but themselves met each year to sell their pelts to the fur companies for the eastern market. They exchanged them for salt and coffee and tea and sugar and clothing and tobacco and whiskey. Without the rendezvous there would have been no established way for them to have disposed of their beaver furs, or to have satisfied the great demand by fashionable eastern gentlemen who needed the luxurious pelts for their tall beaver hats.

The rendezvous was also a giant fiesta.

For a few weeks white men and Indians who spent the rest of their time fighting one another or struggling to live alone in the wilderness forgot their hatreds and the constant dangers of their lives, and had a good time. The Indians came on their finest horses, wearing their most beautifully decorated buckskin breeches and leggings. Their hair was oiled and plaited, or it hung heavy and black about their shoulders.

The white hunters came, so bronzed and weatherbeaten by their long years in the sun and the blizzards that it was almost impossible to tell them from the Indians. Indeed, Narcissa found that the greatest compliment she could pay one of the rough mountain men was to mistake him for an Indian. The mountain men, like their Indian friends, wore long shirts of buckskin fringed with colored porcupine quills, and their hair was long and combed carefully to fall about their shoulders. Most of these lonely men had married Indian women, and they came to the rendezvous, too. Their heavy saddles and the baby cradles which were hung upon the front horn of their saddles were heavily ornamented with beads and bracelets, elk teeth and steel thimbles, rings and shells, which flashed in the sunlight and jingled with each movement.

At evening Narcissa looked about the great encampment, where hundreds of campfires filled the pale blue sky with smoke. There was fighting and drinking and cursing, as the Indians and the white men fought and raced their horses, wrestled and ran foot races, and played games of skill, on horseback and afoot.

When it grew too dark for sport, they settled down by their fires to exchange hair-raising stories of their adventures and narrow escapes. Many of their tales of blizzards and wild animals and starvation needed no embellishment to chill their listeners' blood, but at times their imaginations ran away, and a chance encounter with an ordinary black bear turned into a struggle to the death with a legendary monster. Exaggerated and fantastic as the tall tales of the western frontier may seem to us today, they mirrored faithfully the strangeness and the untamed grandeur of the western mountains and plains and the lonely lives of the mountain men.

Narcissa shivered a little and pressed more closely to Marcus' side as these tales were told around the fires.

"So many of them are such rough men," she said half-fearfully.

"Ah, Narcissa, it often seems that rough men are needed to open a new rough country. You won't see many signs of civilization here. But most of them are really good men. They'd do anything to help a stranger." In spite of their rough characters, Marcus admired the daring mountain men and recognized the importance of their pioneer work in charting the western wilderness.

At last the furs were bartered and the games were finished. The American Fur Company, with its pack animals now heavy with great bales of skins, set forth on the long trip back to St. Louis. The Indians broke their camps and started for their hunting grounds. The trappers prepared their traps and went their way into the mountains for their winter's work. The great site of the rendezvous, which had been crowded and noisy with men and animals, was deserted and silent.

Marcus Whitman had had a great disappointment at the rendezvous. There had been no letter of information and instruction from Dr. Samuel Parker waiting there for him, and he had relied on it to guide his decisions for the rest of the way. From the rendezvous he could no longer travel with the American Fur Company, which had an unwritten but effective understanding with the Hudson's Bay Com-

pany not to engage in business on the western side of
the Rocky Mountains.

Narcissa looked at her husband in dismay when
she realized that they were to go forward without
any help or advice.

"Don't worry, Narcissa," he told her. "God will
watch over us and see that we do the right thing."

As he pressed her hand, his own heart was heavy
within him. Had he brought his bride so far only to
find failure?

They could go on to Oregon with the Nez Percés
but the route would be much longer, for the Indians
would circle to the north where they could find good
hunting, and they would stop along the way. Marcus
wanted to reach Oregon and find a mission site before
the first winter snows. A year's delay in establishing
their mission would not be approved by the American Board, and he and Narcissa were eager, too, to
get to their work.

As he thought over his problem, his brow creased
with worry, a hearty, bluff man strode up to the
campfire where the little band of missionaries were
sitting.

"Nathaniel Wyeth, at your service, ma'am," he said
to Narcissa. "I hear you're planning to go to Oregon.
And a good thing. Good people like yourselves, and
Americans, too, are needed there."

Narcissa stared quite frankly. This was the great
Captain Wyeth, who, it was said, had lost a fortune
when he tried to establish a fur company in Oregon
and was undersold and ruined by the Hudson's Bay
Company. Moreover, here was an American, a friend,
a person who would tell them the truth about Oregon. The things he told them gave them encouragement to continue on the long, weary journey.

"Oregon is a rich fine land," he said. "Why, the
Hudson's Bay Company raises thousands of bushels
of wheat a year just around its forts. The Indians
could raise plenty of crops, too, so that they wouldn't
starve to death every time a hard winter comes along
and there's not much hunting. But somebody has got
to show them how to do it and keep after them until
they do—and the fur company's not likely to do
that."

"Why not, Captain Wyeth?" asked Eliza Spalding,
who was well and strong again and eager to hear of
Oregon.

"Well, ma'am, you know that Spain and Russia and
Great Britain and the United States have all had
claims to the Oregon territory. Russia and Spain have
settled their claims by treaty. But both Great Britain
and the United States have had too much interest in
the country to give up, and they were the only ones
with really strong claims."

"The Lewis and Clark party explored the area for the United States in 1805, didn't it?" asked Henry Spalding.

"Yes," answered Wyeth. "That was really the end of any great exploration, because Lewis and Clark did it pretty thoroughly. That expedition is one of the strongest bases for the American claim. Then John Jacob Astor started his great Pacific Fur Company, founded the town of Astoria, and sent trappers and whole colonies of people out to Oregon. But the War of 1812 with Britain put an end to his project, and after the war he could never get started again. The British Hudson's Bay Company was too well established."

"But I still don't understand why the Hudson's Bay Company wouldn't be likely to teach the Indians to farm," interrupted Eliza.

"Just a minute, ma'am. I'm coming to that. Now, this is what I've been leading up to. You know that according to the treaty we signed in 1818 and renewed in 1827 with Great Britain, the Oregon territory is in joint occupancy. Any American or any Britisher or Canadian should be able to go there and do what he wants. But the Hudson's Bay Company actually controls the country, because they're so strong and can drive others out. It isn't in their interest to teach the Indians to farm, because it might turn them away from trapping furs and that wouldn't be good for the company's business."

"Do you think that the company will try to hinder us in establishing a mission?" asked Marcus in alarm, wondering if that could have been the reason that Dr. Parker hadn't written him detailed instructions.

"No," said Wyeth slowly, scratching his head thoughtfully. "No, I don't think they'll bother American missionaries, although they might discourage general American settlement. They want Oregon to belong to Great Britain when the score is settled. But I think they'll probably help you in nearly every way they can, give you the supplies and the seed that you'll need."

"Well, sir, that is very encouraging to hear. Now all we have to do is find a safe, quick way to get to Oregon," Marcus smiled at Narcissa.

"What?" boomed the captain. "You mean you don't know how you're going to get to Oregon? Well, I can tell you. The Hudson's Bay Company sent Thomas McKay and John McLeod here this year with a party. You're in luck, because usually they don't bother with this rendezvous. I came with them on my way back east. They'll give you plenty of guidance and protection on the way to Oregon. They're going the short route, and you'll be in good hands."

Narcissa smiled with joy. Their problem was solved. They would be in Oregon before the snow fell.

5. THE FIRST WHITE WOMAN

MR. MC KAY AND MR. MC LEOD were happy to offer the protection of their party the rest of the way to Oregon, but they advised Marcus to leave his wagon at the rendezvous. West of the rendezvous they were to enter the high sagebrush country, where it would be increasingly difficult to travel.

This Marcus refused to do. He was determined to take his wagon as far as he could, simply to prove to future emigrants that wagons could travel the trail to Oregon.

Most of the Indians had never seen a wheeled vehicle before, and they were as fascinated as children with a new and wonderful toy. They offered to help Marcus find a passable trail for it as far as they attended the party, for they had insisted on escorting the missionaries over part of the route.

The Indians carried their own supplies packed in

a rawhide pouch hung between two long poles, which were tied to a horse, an ingenious contraption which was called a *travois,* pronounced "tra-vwa." Over the years a rough sort of trail had been made by the passage of these *travois,* and it was over this trail that Marcus planned to take his wagon.

Somehow, with much pushing and pulling, the missionary and his helpers made it to Fort Hall from the rendezvous, and here again he was urged to abandon his precious wagon. Again he refused.

From Fort Hall, the way grew even rougher, and at last, at Fort Boise, where Mr. McKay left the caravan, Marcus realized that he could take the wagon no farther if he planned to reach Oregon in 1836. At the fort, then, he reluctantly left his wheels behind.

When the missionaries left Fort Boise, one of the roughest stages of the journey—but the last—began. Like many later parties, they decided that they should separate so that there would be less demand on their small food supply. They were no longer completely dependent on the dried jerky, for occasionally there was fresh salmon available, but they knew that they had scarcely enough to support all of them at the slow speed at which the footsore cattle forced them to travel.

Marcus and Narcissa Whitman and Mr. Gray went forward with Mr. McLeod's party toward Fort Walla

Walla, the Hudson's Bay Company fort, while the Spaldings, the two Indian boys, and two helpers from the fur company remained behind to bring in the weary cattle.

Through the beautiful Grande Ronde country the advance party hurried to cross the magnificent barrier of the pine-covered Blue Mountains. From the top of this great range they could see the mighty Columbia River valley and, afar, the cone-shaped volcanoes, Mount Hood and Mount St. Helens. Narcissa wrote home, "Behind Mount Hood, the sun was hiding part of his rays, which give us a more distinct view of this gigantic cone. The beauty of this extensive valley contrasted well with the rolling mountains behind us, and at this hour of twilight was enchanting. . . ."

Quickly the vanguard made the sharp and tortuous descent into the valley of the Walla Walla River. On August 29, 1836, Narcissa Whitman looked for the first time upon Waiilatpu, the "place of rye grass," the beautiful land that was to be the scene of her work, of her tragedies, of her happiness, and of her martyrdom.

The first white woman had crossed the great American plains and the Rocky Mountains.

6. OREGON AT LAST

THE DAWN OF THE FIRST DAY of September broke bright and clear. Narcissa and Marcus rose with the first light and quickly prepared the coffee and sliced a roasted duck which one of the hunters had given them. They were excited and hurried as they dressed and broke their camp, for on this day they were to reach Fort Walla Walla, the end of their long and weary months on the trail. Perhaps they would again taste fresh vegetables and fruit and have newly baked white bread instead of fried cakes made from flour and water.

Mr. McLeod had ridden ahead into the fort on the previous day, for, as Narcissa wrote home, "It is the custom of the country to send heralds ahead to announce the arrival of a party, and prepare for their reception." At a gallop Marcus and Narcissa approached the fort; even the weary horses seemed to understand that this was the end of the trail.

49

Out of the fort to meet them rode a gay welcoming party—Mr. McLeod, Mr. Pambrun, who was the Hudson's Bay Company's factor in charge of Fort Walla Walla, and a Mr. Townsend, a traveling naturalist.

At the log and adobe fort Narcissa looked about with delight. A young rooster crowed from the sill of a door. Flocks of hens and turkeys and pigeons scratched in the dirt. Cows and goats browsed quietly on the few scant patches of grass. On the table a plentiful breakfast of fresh salmon and potatoes and tea and fresh white bread and butter was spread for Marcus and Narcissa by Mrs. Pambrun, who was an Indian woman. To their wondering eyes, it seemed a feast.

After breakfast they were shown to their quarters, where a startling surprise awaited the gentle Narcissa. Their room was the west bastion of the fort, with portholes, instead of windows, in the walls, and it was filled with firearms. There was even a cannon by their bed.

But the cannon, which stood always loaded to remind them that they were in unknown and sometimes treacherous country, did not disturb their rest. At last Marcus and Narcissa had a roof to shield them from the hot Oregon sun and a rough but real bed, instead of the India rubber cloth and their blankets laid upon the hard ground.

Two days later, the Spaldings, with their helpers, arrived with the cattle. Eliza Spalding was now in good health, so good indeed that she decided to join the rest of the party in the trip down the river to Fort Vancouver, where they hoped to find Dr. Samuel Parker and to make friendly arrangements for their mission with Dr. John McLoughlin, chief factor, or manager, of the Hudson's Bay Company.

On Sunday, when the missionaries gathered together for their first worship in the new land, Narcissa's heart welled with great thanksgiving that they had been allowed to travel safely through the dangerous wastes and mountains to this great territory. She looked affectionately at her sturdy husband, his face shining with the light of dedication to the work of God.

She knew that, on this same day, her loved ones were gathered together back in the States, and that their thoughts, too, were with her and Marcus and that their prayers were offered for their safekeeping and their chosen labor.

Humbly she bowed her head and prayed silently

that she be given the strength and the courage and the human understanding to obey faithfully the great command of Christ: "Go ye into all the world, and preach the gospel to every creature."

7. THE PLACE OF
RYE GRASS

ON SEPTEMBER 6, the following Wednesday, Narcissa and Marcus and the Spaldings set out down the Columbia for Fort Vancouver. They were traveling with Factor Pambrun, for Mr. McLeod had left Walla Walla several days before. Narcissa enjoyed the restful journey by water in the open boat, which was manned by six oarsmen.

To her family she wrote, ". . . it is a very pleasant change in our manner of travelling. The Columbia is a beautiful river. Its waters are clear as crystal and smooth as a sea of glass. . . . There is no timber to be seen, but there are high perpendicular banks of rocks in some places, while rugged bluffs and plains of sand in others, are all that greet the eye."

At the Chute, a fall in the river, she saw for the first time how a portage was made. In a matter of minutes, the baggage was loaded on the backs of some of the Indians who had been waiting at the Chute to help the party, and the boat was capsized and placed on the heads of about twenty others, who carried it overland around the impassable Chute.

Narcissa and Marcus walked slowly through the masses of broken rock, staring with amazement at the narrow channels and the steep precipices.

"You should see it when the water is high," Mr. Pambrun told them. "Then all of these rocks are covered with water."

A few more miles down the river were the Dalles, two immense rocks which blocked the stream so that the river was forced between them in a channel so narrow that again a portage had to be made.

While the boat was being unloaded, Marcus decided to walk to the top of a large rock to watch the river. Narcissa waited for him at the base. She watched him climb for a moment and then sat down to rest and to eat some hazelnuts she had with her. There was a strange prickling on her neck. She put her hand under her cape to investigate and brought it away with two insects upon it. Fleas! Jumping up, she looked at her cape, her dress. She was covered with fleas, scrambling for her bare face and neck! Frantically she shook herself, and then she tried to climb the rock after Marcus. But he had seen her frenzied motion and was soon at her side. Together, they shook and brushed for an hour, but not until she reached the boat again and washed and changed her clothes did she feel comfortable. A few sly, embarrassed glances at the other passengers and the oarsmen showed her that all were suffering.

When the missionaries ended their river trip at Vancouver, they received a hearty welcome from Dr. McLoughlin of the Hudson's Bay Company. But, to their disappointment, Dr. Parker had gone back to the United States by way of the Hawaiian Islands. He had not left any letter of advice for them, but he had made many friends who were eager to aid the American missionaries.

At Vancouver, Marcus and Narcissa enjoyed seeing the bustling fort and the surrounding country. They admired the great orchards of apples, peaches, pears, and plums, and the huge gardens with cucumbers, melons, beans, peas, cabbage, tomatoes, every kind of fresh vegetable. They visited the large farm, with its hundreds of cattle, sheep, and goats, and with its wheat and barley and oat fields, from which the fur company expected great returns. And in the Vancouver stores Narcissa found none of the luxuries of life, but most of the things which she would need to start her home and housekeeping.

She and Marcus smiled at each other in wondering pleasure over the lush fields and gardens. They knew

now that they had come to a truly rich country, a
land which would yield greatly to those who had the
courage and the energy to enter it and settle it. With
high hearts they discussed the immense work to be
done. They must build their mission, plant the crops
which they would need for themselves and for those
who turned to them for help, and show the nomadic
Indians the great rewards of agriculture and settled
living. Above all, they must devote their hearts and
energies to bringing the natives an understanding of
the teachings of the Bible and the worship of God.

After a few days of rest in Fort Vancouver, Marcus
and Henry Spalding returned up the Columbia to se-
lect sites for their missions. It had been decided that
two stations should be established, for both the Nez
Percé and the Cayuse tribes wanted missionaries to
settle permanently among them.

On this exploratory trip, Marcus decided to settle
among the Cayuse, a small tribe which at this time
had only some three hundred members, on the Walla
Walla River, in Waiilatpu. This location was directly
on the best route from the east. Henry Spalding selected a spot in the Nez Percé country, in what is
now western Idaho.

Marcus stayed at Waiilatpu to start the building of
his home for Narcissa, for winter was by now close
on their heels, while Henry Spalding returned to Van-

couver to bring back Narcissa and Eliza and the supplies which they would need.

"You should spend the winter with us, Mrs. Whitman," Dr. McLoughlin protested. "By next spring
your husband will have built your house, and it will
be much easier for you. We can promise you good
company here, and much more comfortable living
than you will find now in the Place of Rye Grass."

"You are very kind, Dr. McLoughlin," Narcissa
replied. "But I feel that I must be with my husband.
Our work must begin now, and there are many things
that I can do to help him, even with the building."

Dr. McLoughlin and the women who lived at the
fort were mostly concerned with the fact that Narcissa was going to have a baby. They felt—although
Narcissa refused to listen—that it would be much
better for her to stay where she would have comfortable quarters and good food to eat, rather than to
go off again into the wilderness to face unpleasant-
ness and possibly even danger.

At Fort Walla Walla, too, Factor Pambrun and his
wife insisted that she spend the winter with them,
but when Marcus came to the fort for his wife, she
turned a grateful but deaf ear to their pleas and went
with him. On December 10 they reached Waiilatpu
together and looked at the lovely peninsula formed
by the two branches of the Walla Walla River. It was

here that their simple house stood. There were trees along the river, and, in the distance, the beautiful Blue Mountains reached toward the sky.

Carefully Marcus helped his wife into the house that he was building for her. He hoped that he had done the right thing when he had encouraged her to come to Waiilatpu for this winter. She was pale and tired as she sat down gratefully upon the box which had become their chair. But she smiled into his eyes and looked about the rough room with curiosity and delight. This was their first home together, and rude as it was, it filled her heart with warm pleasure.

There was a great fireplace and chimney, but there was no furniture except for the chair made from the box and the table fashioned from a packing case. There was a floor, but blankets were nailed over the openings where someday windows would be. There was no bed, except for green cottonwood branches laid on the floor and covered with quilts.

Marcus watched her anxiously. "My dear, I hope that you never have reason to regret—" he began.

Narcissa broke in, "Oh, no, Marcus. Never, never will I be sorry that I have come. We have the prayers of those at home helping us. I know that they are thinking of us, even at this moment. And the Lord will help us and give us strength."

Marcus Whitman and his wife knelt together to

pray for God's guidance—knelt together for the first time in their new home, far from their kinfolk, far from friendly neighbors, surrounded only by strange country and by unknown Indians.

8. CAYUSE *TE-MI*

IN A FEW DAYS THE FIRST SNOW FELL, and Narcissa found herself winter-bound. Food ran short, for she had only the supplies that she had brought from Vancouver and Fort Walla Walla. Marcus killed a horse, and, for the first time, Narcissa feasted on horse meat. Their few cattle had to be kept for breeding stock, but Oregon's great herds of wild horses were to supply much of their meat. It was, indeed, to be several years before a beef—a dry and stringy old cow—was killed, and several more years before horse meat disappeared completely from their table.

The deep snow was a great help to Marcus, for it enabled him to drag timber from the Blue Mountains, some fifteen miles away, timber which he needed badly for building and for fuel. When there was no snow, it was tedious and slow work to bring the logs down to the mission over the rough ground.

These first days were busy ones for Marcus and Narcissa. Besides laboring to complete their little house, they began at once to work with the Indians, for both of them were anxious to learn the language of the Cayuse and to teach some of the Indians to speak English. Not until they were able to talk to the Indians could they begin to teach them the Bible and to explain Christ's great commandments for men to love God and to love their neighbor.

Narcissa quickly organized a school for the Indian children in her little house. As the weeks passed, she longed for a larger place. The Indian braves and squaws crowded into her kitchen while she was trying to cook and clean or teach. They were very dirty. Each time after they had visited, she had to scrub and sweep to rid herself of the mud and fleas they had brought in. She knew that she had to set a good example. She had not come to their lonely land to adopt their careless ways of living but to teach them how to be clean and healthy. Cleanliness was, indeed, next to godliness, she thought to herself, as she busily scrubbed the rough wooden floor.

More quickly than they had dared to hope, Marcus and Narcissa were able to speak the Indian language well enough to begin services on the Sabbath.

The Indians spent a good part of their time away from their villages near the mission. In winter they went to their regular winter quarters, but with the coming of spring they returned, to see after what little planting they had, to hunt for the edible biscuit root, which they dried and stored, and to set their simple weblike traps for the spring salmon run. During the later part of the summer and the early fall, many Indians were away from the mission on their annual buffalo hunt, but late fall found most of them back in their lodges, preparing their supplies for the siege of winter.

To the missionaries this nomadic life, orderly as it was in its yearly cycle, presented a serious problem, since it made daily contact and constant activity with most of the Indians almost impossible. But Marcus and Narcissa did the best they could with their fluctuating congregation.

During the winter, when only fifty or sixty Indians remained nearby, Sabbath services were held in the Whitmans' own home. On nice days during the spring, summer, and fall, when a large group of Indians attended, Marcus held the services out of doors in a grassy clearing, but on rainy days, a Cayuse lodge, large enough for the crowding Indians, became his church.

Often several families would join their lodges, which were made of skins and rush mats, to make a long and roomy chamber. In the center there was a fire, and the smoke escaped through a hole cut in the roof.

Marcus soon found a very successful way to preach to the Cayuse. He would invite one of the most interested and intelligent of the Indians to study with him on the evening before the Sabbath. During the lesson he would translate the text of Scripture that he had chosen for the Sunday service and then explain it to the Indian until he understood completely.

Then the next morning, after the hymn, Marcus would read the text and begin his sermon. After each sentence, the Indian whom he had taught the night before would translate it to the congregation. This ceremonious repetition was used by the Cayuse in their great tribal rituals and councils, and Marcus found that they listened with greater respect and seemed to understand better his preaching of Christ's message when he copied their fashion.

The Cayuse, Marcus found, loved to listen to the singing of the stately hymns and to join in as soon as they could. They loved to have him tell them the dramatic and beautiful stories of the Bible, and to read the Ten Commandments. These they would repeat over and over again, as a sort of magic. But they did not like him to tell them that they had bad hearts and that they did wicked things.

"You are a bad man," they would say sullenly and

angrily, when Marcus sternly rebuked them for being unkind to their neighbors or for fighting and
killing.

The Cayuse were a proud and impudent people
whose tribal history was filled with tales of blood-
shed and wanton cruelty to the neighboring tribes.
Because of their many wars, few of the young men
lived to old age, and slowly the numbers of the tribe
had grown less, for with each generation there were
fewer children. But they had not grown less fierce in
their tribal pride.

"The Nez Percés warned us against settling here,"
said Marcus to his wife one evening. "And I see why.
These Cayuse are hard to live with. They have picked
up the white man's bad habits, but they haven't copied his good ones. Old Chief Umtippe is about the
worst of the lot, and we must deal with him most of
the time. Perhaps when the old ones die, we will be
able to work better with the young braves."

"Umtippe was here today," Narcissa replied, turning from her dishwashing. "He was complaining that
you should pay him for the land we're living on, and
he said that I should give him presents."

"That's the way they are. If you do something for
one of them, all of them beg for gifts. They seem to
think you're under obligation to them if you give
them a dose of medicine. Umtippe's angry, too, be-

cause we're teaching the young people and the children. He says that he is chief, and that I should teach only him. If I teach the common Indians, he's afraid they will lose respect for him. Why, he even ordered them not to talk with us, because he's afraid we'll pick up a few words."

"Well, Marcus, I know one bad habit of the white man's that they haven't picked up yet," Narcissa said laughingly. "They don't steal. The Indians east of the Rocky Mountains do. Here I can leave the laundry on the line, and not so much as a handkerchief will be taken."

She paused and watched Marcus's tired, solemn face. "We mustn't let ourselves become discouraged at the very start, Marcus. I feel in my heart that God will help us. Some of them do seem to be interested and to want to learn."

Marcus sighed. "I know we mustn't get discouraged. But when I think of trying to teach them to plant and to build irrigation ditches and to keep their crops in order, I wonder how we will ever do it. They really hate work. All they want to do is hunt buffalo, and dig up that camas root they eat and fish for salmon. They think that a man is a slave if he does any real work, and they don't like it when I keep after them for help. It's no wonder that they starve to death and catch every disease that comes along.

As long as they have some horses—and there's one old fellow who owns several thousand—they don't care about anything."

"I know they think you are foolish to help me around the house and to do the heavy work at the mission. They must be afraid that you'll set a bad example and that their wives will be chasing them with a tomahawk."

Marcus laughed and patted her hand. "Well, I'm going to keep right on helping you. You must take every care of yourself, especially until the baby comes. After that, you'll really have plenty to do."

On March 14, 1837, Narcissa's own birthday, a little girl was born to Narcissa and Marcus. They named her Alice Clarissa, after her two grandmothers.

The Cayuse Indians were delighted with her. Men, women, and children crowded into the tiny room where Narcissa lay with her, to stare at her fair skin and light brown hair and blue eyes, and to wonder loudly why Narcissa did not bind her head to a board after their fashion so that she would grow up to be beautiful. They were very proud that the first white baby to be born in Oregon should be born on *Cayuse Wai-tis,* Cayuse land, and they named her *Cayuse te-mi,* Cayuse girl.

As Narcissa looked fondly at her child, and then about at the admiring savage faces, she realized how hard it would be to rear her properly far from white civilization and among the barbaric Indians, who would surely have an influence on the little girl. She wrote to her family: "To be a mother in heathen land, among savages, gives feelings that can be known only to those who are such. . . . Ye mothers . . . let me beg an interest in your prayers, especially for your un-worthy sister, now she has become a mother, and for my little one."

But the little *Cayuse te-mi* yawned and smiled and played and cried and grew rapidly, unconscious of the anxious heart of her mother.

9. *TE-WAT* WHITMAN

FOR A TIME AFTER THE BIRTH of Alice Clarissa, the Indians did not quarrel with her mother and father. Their hearts seemed to have been made kindly by the beautiful little girl, and they listened to her parents with greater interest.

Marcus and Narcissa felt that the gentle words of Christ were beginning to have an effect. But this truce, for that was all it was, did not last.

Early in April, just before spring planting was to be started, an epidemic of what Marcus called "inflammation of the lungs" struck the Indian villages, and Marcus' work was doubled. At first, the Cayuse were grateful to him for his help and good nursing, but there were those among them who muttered that the ancient tribal ways of treating sickness were better and that the white *te-wat*, the medicine man, would bring death to their tents.

The western Indians, like many primitive people, did not understand that sickness should be treated with medicine and rest and proper nursing. They thought that a person fell sick when his enemy hired a powerful *te-wat* to cast a magic spell on him, and that the only way to cure this evil magic was to hire an even more powerful *te-wat* to throw an even more powerful spell that would overcome the sickness.

The *te-wat*, dressed in strange clothing and wearing horrible masks, would chant and dance over the sick person until the devil which plagued him would disappear with fright. Then the person would be well.

This superstition grew out of the Indians' overpowering fear of the unseen. They feared anything unknown, such as a new country or a new tribe, and above all, they feared death.

Although they talked boastingly of their bravery at a council meeting or at the rendezvous, before a battle they held war dances which would excite them so that they would forget they were afraid. In sickness, particularly in one which made many of their people ill, they called on the *te-wat* to excite them with his dances and chants and frightful masks so that they could forget their own fears.

Surrounded by natural forces which they did not understand, the Cayuse believed that all animals—

mammals or snakes or fish—had once been men and
that these creatures still spoke the language of that
long-lost race. If a man could come to understand
this language, he would be in favor with the creatures and be given miraculous powers, both for good
and evil.

When a boy approached manhood, it was required
that he spend several days alone in the mountains
without food or water, waiting for the supernatural
animals to speak to him. Of these boys, some few
were received with special honor by the gods, and if
these few could prove their new powers, they were
accepted as *te-wats*.

It was a great honor to be a *te-wat*, even greater
than to be a chief, and many of the young men did
foolish things to prove that they had unusual powers
and could control the unknown spirits that ruled the
world of nature. One young man among the Cayuse
shot himself through the body because he wanted to
convince his tribe that he controlled the spirits. After
a quick recovery, he was considered one of the most
powerful of medicine men and was called in during
serious illnesses.

But even though it was a great honor to be a *te-
wat*, it was also a very dangerous calling. Often a
te-wat would say that a sick man was well and would
receive his pay of horses and clothing and bullets.

Then the man would die, and, in revenge, his friends would seek out the *te-wat* and kill him. Indian justice was swift and merciless.

The Indians, who had learned these superstitions in babyhood, could not understand that Marcus Whitman was a doctor, who treated their sicknesses with medicines and good nursing, instead of magic. They thought that he was just another *te-wat*, although perhaps more powerful than any other, and that it was always his fault if his patient died.

During the terrible spring epidemic of lung trouble, Marcus was called to the sick wife of Umtippe, the Cayuse chief who had demanded payment for the mission land, and Umtippe threatened to kill the doctor if his wife died.

But at last the epidemic passed, and Marcus was safe, for all of those whom he had treated recovered quickly. When old Chief Umtippe himself fell sick, he sent for the white *te-wat*—high praise for Marcus' powers as a medicine man.

"We must indeed thank God that none of our patients died," Marcus told Narcissa. "It is just a superstition like this that could destroy all of our usefulness. Perhaps I must die among these Indians. But I want first to accomplish something that will help them. I am afraid that they are going to die out as a tribe. Disease and starvation and their wars will eventually destroy them. I would like to teach them about the salvation of Christ, so that they may face death without fear. Some of them will live, and they will be the ones who will learn our teachings and form a strong Christian group among the Indians."

"Brother Spalding doesn't have as much trouble with his Nez Percés as we have here. They seem much more willing to listen to him and to try to understand the Bible. Oh, Marcus, I sometimes wish that we had never settled here among the Cayuse. I dread to think of the danger that you are always in," cried Narcissa.

"My dear, it is for that reason that we are so needed here," answered her husband. "The Cayuse must be shown the love of God. Until the Indians kill me or drive us out, we shall stay and work."

10. TROUBLE WITH THE INDIANS

TROUBLES WITH THE INDIANS came and went as the years passed by. At times, Marcus and Narcissa could rejoice over steady progress in their religious teaching, but often they were downcast by a serious failure.

An alphabet for the Nez Percé language, which was also spoken by the Cayuse, was devised and a schoolbook was written in the Indian tongue. When a printing press was sent from the Sandwich Islands, this book was printed, and the Indians were delighted to learn to read in their own language.

Narcissa taught her school of Indian children and tried to manage her household at the same time. She was constantly busy and harried because the mission had become the stopping place for all those migrating into Oregon. Often families with no food and clothing sought shelter with her and Marcus, and sometimes stayed for months. Her days were filled,

too, with the unending demands of the Indians, who
stared unblinkingly through the doors and the windows, and who tramped into her house, imperiously
ordering her to give them presents and food.

At times it was more than Narcissa could endure,
and she and little Alice Clarissa often went with
Marcus on his trips away from the mission. Once she
and Marcus, with the baby, accompanied the Cayuse
on their annual hunt and lived in the rude skin te-
pees, in order to spend more time in close compan-
ionship with the elusive Indians.

In the spring of 1840, Narcissa's greatest wish
came true. Marcus was at last able to finish a larger
and roomier house than the little hut they had been
living in. A bigger place had become absolutely necessary because of the great amount of company they
had with them almost constantly.

Valuable help had arrived in the spring of 1838
from the American Board. Mr. Gray, who had returned to the East, brought back with him his lovely
bride, three missionary families, and one bachelor
missionary.

Help was desperately needed, for Marcus was
seriously overburdened. He had tried to teach the
Cayuse and to nurse them in sickness and to work
on the mission buildings and the farm, until he was
nearly exhausted. His brown hair, although he was

in his middle thirties, had become heavily streaked with gray. An old back-trouble had returned, but he had driven himself uncomplainingly to his work. Narcissa and Marcus knew that they had to raise enough grain and potatoes and vegetables to keep them all through the winter and to help the other missionaries and the families who passed by the station. They had to raise plentiful crops, for their allowance from the American Board was only five hundred dollars a year. This small amount—although the value of five hundred dollars meant far more then in terms of what it would buy than it does today— had to cover both their personal needs and the heavy mission expenses.

The new missionaries were heartily welcomed. At last, perhaps, more could be accomplished.

"We feel," wrote Marcus to Dr. David Greene, the secretary of the American Board, "like St. Paul when he met the brethren from Rome: we thank God and take courage."

Among the Indians, however, anger was growing. They did not approve of Marcus' plan to teach them to farm, and they thought that his fine new house meant that he was growing rich from the produce of Cayuse land. They did not understand that Marcus and Narcissa did not own any of the mission build-

ings, and they had forgotten their earnest invitation
to the missionaries to live among them.

The Indians wanted to hold the Sabbath services
in the Whitmans' new house, and they wished to be
free to come and go as they liked inside the house,
for it was built on their land. Marcus urged them to
build their own large lodge for the services and told
them that among the white men there were separate
houses for the worship of God.

In the new house there was a room kept especially
for visits from the Indians, but they regarded this as
an insult and insisted upon entering into the kitchen
and the living rooms of the family.

Fueled by these serious resentments, their anger
came to a boil in November, 1841.

Marcus was far from being a weakling or a cow-
ard. When his position as the missionary of God was
insulted, his temper often blazed up, and he would
face down the most treacherous Indian. But during
the troubles of the fall of 1841, he again and again
showed the Indians the meaning of the words of
Jesus: ". . . resist not evil: . . . whosoever shall smite
thee on thy right cheek, turn to him the other also."

The chief troublemaker was a young Indian named
Tilaukait, who was to play another and a more terrible part in the Whitmans' life in later years. Tilaukait, looking for trouble, turned his horses into the

unfenced corn and potato fields of the mission to graze. Marcus simply had the horses led off by other Indians who were helping him.

A short time later, as Marcus stood watching Mr. Gray, who was working with him at the time on the ditches being dug around the fields for irrigation and protection, Tilaukait appeared, his face angry.

"I will whip Indians you send to lead off horses," he threatened Marcus. "I will take one of your horses, too, for hunt and leave him far away."

"This land is for farming, Tilaukait," Marcus replied calmly. "It is not a horse pen, and you keep your horses out of it."

"This is my land, *te-wat*. You have no right here unless you pay. What do you pay for land?"

"I have paid nothing, and I will never pay anything. Your people invited us to live here and said that we could live without paying."

"Shame, shame. You bad."

But Marcus, trying to control his anger, turned away.

Near the house another Indian stopped him to ask about the quarrel. As they talked, Tilaukait came up behind Marcus and struck him without warning.

"Stop talking, bad man!" he ordered.

Marcus looked at him. "I have been talking since

my childhood," he replied, "and I intend to keep on doing so."

Then he went quietly into the house.

A few days later, Tilaukait, finding himself unable to get any satisfaction from Marcus, picked a quarrel with Mr. Gray, who was working on his own house. Mr. Gray had ordered another young Indian out of the kitchen. The Indian went at once and stole one of the mission's horses, but Gray, who had followed him, took his rope from the horse and put the brave out of the horse pen.

Shortly, Tilaukait appeared and ordered Gray to stop work on the house and to leave.

"It is the Sabbath," said Marcus who had hurried to Gray as soon as he heard of the new quarrel, "and he cannot leave."

"Let him stop work, for he is working for nothing," Tilaukait insisted.

"We believe in working, and we will work even if it turns out to be for nothing," replied Marcus.

"You are helping Gray. And he is bad man who will not let Indian in house."

"That is our house, and we have the right to put out somebody who does not belong there."

Tilaukait stepped forward, pulled Marcus' ear and struck him on the chest again and again. When Marcus did nothing but turn the other ear toward him, he jerked off the doctor's hat and threw it in the mud. Three times he did this, and each time Marcus waited until one of the helping Indians brought it to him and put it on again, dripping with water and mud.

"You must be playing," said Marcus, a faint smile on his lips.

Tilaukait, angry but puzzled by the white man's calmness, turned away.

"I intend to ignore the whole thing," Marcus said to Narcissa later. "These Indians are more like children than men, and so we must treat them like children with a tantrum."

But they were not allowed to ignore it. News of the trouble had reached Fort Walla Walla, which was now under the command of Archibald McKinlay. He sent for the Indians and told them that the Hudson's Bay Company did not build forts and buy skins and bring supplies to the Indians to have the white people injured. If they behaved like dogs—and this was the greatest insult he could offer the Indians— the company would certainly see that they were punished.

Many of the Indians were greatly excited and upset by this threat. They came to the mission house and ordered Narcissa, who was alone in the house, to call Marcus.

Through the kitchen several of the Indians came,

into the dining room, and seated themselves. One old brave shook a hammer at Narcissa through the window and ordered her to open the doors so that all of them could enter. Marcus managed to lock the doors, but the Indians, with a hammer and an axe, knocked down these flimsy barriers and rushed in, trying to strike Marcus and Gray with their tools. They were disarmed.

Another Indian attacked Marcus with a club, but Marcus forced it from his grasp.

"You are afraid to die," he contemptuously said to Marcus.

"I am not afraid to die, but I do not intend to sin by helping someone to kill me. I will defend myself as best I can."

"You must not close any doors against us any more," interrupted another Cayuse. "And you must give us presents. That is what fur company do when there is any trouble."

"We will always lock our doors and protect our house," replied Marcus. "And I will not give any presents to you for being bad. You must learn to have better hearts."

Finally the Indians left, muttering angrily among themselves.

In the morning the Indians were still angry. It was Sunday, and Marcus held church services in spite of the danger, but most of the Cayuse refused to attend. Others came carrying their weapons. During the day they broke the windows in the house and troubled the horses and cattle.

"We must barricade ourselves tonight," Marcus said softly to Narcissa, who was holding Alice in her lap and trying to be calm. "This looks like really serious trouble, and I think we've turned the other cheek long enough. If they attack us, and I wouldn't be surprised if they do, we must defend ourselves. Tomorrow, if we're still alive, we'll go to the fort and ask for protection."

Somehow the night passed, although the missionaries stayed awake all of the time, listening for every noise that might mean attack. But on Monday there was a letter from McKinlay to tell them that they would have no more trouble. He had talked to the Indians again and threatened them with the anger of the Hudson's Bay Company. He had told the Indians, he wrote, "that I knew they might kill you before assistance came, but that it afforded me great satisfaction they could not send you to hell. That it is the first time I have heard of Indians in any part of the country treating missionaries so, and that I never heard in any country of missionaries being obliged to pay for the lands they occupied. I concluded by saying that if they were willing to acknowledge their faults and promise better conduct in the future, I was sure you would forgive the past and that if you did I would do so, also. . . . one and all of them . . . expressed deep contrition for what had passed and many promises that they would conduct themselves well in the future."

When he had read the letter, Marcus called the Indians together and told them that he wanted to forgive them, but that they must promise to behave better in the days to come.

"We did not come so far to fight with you," he said sadly. "We came to teach you the word of God and to help you in your sickness and trouble. But if you do not promise to help us, too, we must leave you. If you decide that we should go, we shall do as you wish, for we can do you no good."

"No, no, we are sorry," several of the Indians who had been ringleaders in the quarrel cried. "Do not leave us. Stay and teach."

There was still a few angry faces in the crowd, but no one dared say anything.

"Well, that is over, for at least a while," said Marcus to Narcissa later. "I hope we shall have peace."

"I know, my dear. It has been a frightening time. I sometimes feel that we shall die here, that we shall be murdered and never see our families and friends again. But the Indians say they want us to stay, and

I think they mean it. As long as we can, we must stay and work with them without fear."

Her words were brave. But often Narcissa waked in the night from a dream of frightful horror and massacre. She would touch her sleeping husband to reassure herself that he was alive.

Although fear was often her companion, she never spoke of turning back from the barbaric country to which she had come. This was the life to which God had called her and which she had accepted, and the fear in her heart was overcome by her courage and her unwavering faith in God's mercy.

11. ALICE CLARISSA

THE BABY, ALICE CLARISSA, was the joy of Narcissa's life. She was strong and healthy and quick to learn. During Marcus' many long absences, when he went to help at the Indian villages or in the distant missions, she was her mother's companion.

The Indians, too, loved her and treated her with gentleness even when they were quarreling with her father and mother. One old Indian told Narcissa that he would leave his land and horses to Alice when he died.

Narcissa had been particularly anxious to rear her little daughter to know the teachings of Jesus and to obey his commandments, for she knew that in this savage country, where there were few white people, it would be easy for Alice to copy the Indian customs. But the little girl was obedient and affectionate. She grew soon into a sturdy, talkative little tod-

dler, who loved to sing and to recite her A B C's and
who could speak with the Indians in their own tongue
better than her parents.

At night, kneeling by her bed, Narcissa prayed,
"Lord, bless little Alice; may she be Thy child, may
she love Thee, and when she dies, may she go to
heaven and live with Jesus, and sing his praises, forever and ever. Amen."

Narcissa knew that there was little danger for her
daughter in Waiilatpu except for the Walla Walla
River, which flowed near the mission house, and she
and Marcus had taught the child to fear it and to
stay away from the water unless one of them was
with her. Watching older children, though, as they
played along the banks, Alice slowly lost her timidity.

One Friday Marcus and Narcissa found her washing a radish in the river, a radish which her father
had just pulled from the garden and then dropped
on the ground.

Narcissa was frightened.

"She is no longer afraid," she whispered to Marcus, as they walked back to the house, Alice trotting
a little before them. "We must try to explain to her
what might happen if she fell in."

"Darling," Marcus said, taking the little girl on his
knee when they had sat down before the fireplace.

"Darling, you remember that I had to drown your little dog the other day, because he was sick and unhappy. Now Boxer went away and left you all alone. If you should fall into the river, you would drown just as he did. Then Mamma and Papa would have no little Alice to sit on their laps."

Alice listened carefully, looking into her father's eyes. She ran to her mother and climbed into her lap to hug her.

"Alice fall in water, Alice she die like Boxer—Mamma have no Alice," she said, looking anxiously at her mother.

Narcissa kissed her. "That is right, dear Alice. You must mind Mamma and Papa and stay away from the river. Whatever would Mamma do with no Alice to play with her?"

On the following Sunday, at the regular service with the Indians, "Rock of Ages" was sung. It was one of the Indians' favorite hymns, and it was little Alice's favorite, too. Narcissa watched her happy little daughter joining in the beautiful hymn and wondered if she did not perhaps love her too much. As she had done many times in the past, she silently prayed again to God that she would be a good mother to Alice and rear her to be a fine and noble woman.

The child's clear voice soared:

While I draw this fleeting breath,
When my eyelids close in death;
When I rise to worlds unknown,
And behold Thee on Thy throne,
Rock of Ages, cleft for me,
Let me hide myself in Thee.

Later that Sunday afternoon Narcissa and Marcus sat reading in the living room while Alice played in and out of the door. Narcissa called to Margaret, the teen-age daughter of Thomas McKay of the Hudson's Bay Company, with whose party the Whitmans had traveled on the way to Oregon. Margaret was living with her and helping with the housekeeping. She told the girl to set the table for supper.

In a few minutes Alice came in and saw the table set.

"Mamma," she cried gaily, "supper is almost ready. Let Alice get some water."

Her parents, engrossed in their books, hardly noticed what she said or did. Singing happily, she took two cups from the table and went out of the door.

In a moment Narcissa missed her gay laughter and play.

"Margaret, please look for Alice. Supper is almost ready."

Margaret looked for her, but could not find her.

Then, instead of returning to tell Narcissa that Alice was nowhere about, she went into the garden to gather some radishes for supper.

Mungo, one of the Whitmans' Hawaiian servants, came in to tell Marcus that there were two cups floating in the river.

"Leave them there, since this is the Sabbath. We can fish them out tomorrow," said Marcus.

"How could cups have gotten there?" cried Narcissa.

"I suppose Alice put them there."

Then Marcus and Narcissa stared at each other.

Narcissa rose to her feet and ran out of the house.

"Alice, Alice," she called, but there was no answer. None of the Indians around the house had seen her. Marcus and Narcissa, terrified by now, rushed down to the river, followed by Mungo and Margaret and some of the Indians. They went up and down the bank and crossed the river, while the Indians jumped into the current and waded downstream, calling and searching for a glimpse of Alice's dress.

Suddenly, an old Indian who had entered the river called, "She is found." A moment later he dragged her dripping body from the spot where she had fallen in.

Marcus reached her first, his face desperate. As he pulled her dress from her face, she seemed to breathe.

But it was too late. For a long time they tried to bring life into her body, but Alice Clarissa Whitman, only a little over two years old, was dead.

Narcissa bowed her head over her child's body. The tears streamed down her face and her body shook with sobs.

"Lord, it is right. It is right. She is not mine, but thine. She has only been lent to me for a little season, and now, dearest Saviour, thou hast the best right to her. Thy will be done, not mine."

12. WAIILATPU IS TO BE ABANDONED

SOMEHOW THE MONTHS after Alice's death passed for Narcissa. She kept herself busy with her household chores and with her teaching; she went with Marcus on his trips to distant villages and missions.

But at last the day came when he had to leave her at home alone. The house was empty and quiet without Alice's gay chatter. Sometimes, bent over her sewing or her reading, trying to work with eyes that burned and ached, Narcissa lifted her head at the creak of a board, her eyes bright again, a smile on her lips, half expecting to find Alice at her elbow.

Slowly, as the months dragged on, her feeling that her great sorrow was only a bad dream faded, and into her saddened heart she took the knowledge that her little daughter had gone forever.

There were to be many cruel reminders for years to come. Clothes and shoes she had ordered, presents and congratulations from friends and relatives, were to arrive months, even years later, because of the very slow communication between Oregon and the eastern states.

Marcus was tender and understanding during their months of grief, but he had many serious problems on his mind. There were, of course, the usual minor quarrels with the Indians, but these were troubles that he had learned to expect and had steeled himself to endure. What he had not expected was the steady bickering among the missionaries themselves.

Many an evening he sat discouraged by the fire, wondering if the good work was to be ruined by the jealousy he found among his co-workers.

"I find it hard to believe that the Lord will foster a ministry when it is hindered by such arguments as we have among us," he said bitterly to Narcissa.

Narcissa sighed. "You know that Henry Spalding and I had a quarrel long, long ago when we were in school together. Father called us both in and made us promise that we would forget the past before he would even agree to my marrying you and coming to the mission. Now Henry seems to want to bring the whole matter up again and keeps telling the others that they must 'expose my character,' as though I were some wicked woman who was trying to ruin the whole missionary work."

"You have had to put up with a lot of foolish gossip, Narcissa. But the worst thing for our work is his jealousy of my position. He hates to think that most of the missionaries look to Waiilatpu as the center of the mission. Here we are, placed squarely on the trail into Oregon. The newcomers pass by here, although there are not so many of them yet. But we must serve them and give them food and clothing after that terrible trip."

"If it would mean peace among the missionaries," Narcissa suggested, "perhaps we could turn this mission over to someone else."

"I have offered to, again and again," answered her husband. "I don't care who is head of Waiilatpu. I have far more than I can do. I simply do not see how much longer I can go on as a doctor and a teacher, too. I can't devote the time I should to the Indians when I'm away for weeks on end seeing after sick people. And that throws too much of the burden on you. I've asked for help—preachers, farmers, teachers—time and again, but the Board doesn't feel that it can take on added expense right now."

"The Board will not be very impressed with our progress when it hears that we don't seem to be able to work together," said Narcissa. "They are experienced men, and they know that quarrels can destroy all that we have tried to do, because the Indians will

soon know all about it. They will have a good joke
on the Christian missionaries." There was a note of
weary despondency in her words.

This was one of Marcus' worries, too. "If the Board
thinks that these arguments and jealousies are serious, they will probably disband the mission," he said.

"Oh, no, Marcus, surely not that!"

But Marcus was right.

In February, 1842, a letter was sent to the Oregon
mission from the Board in Boston ordering the dis-
missal of Mr. Spalding and two other mission workers and sending Marcus into the northern part of the
country. This meant that Waiilatpu was to be abandoned. Faced with increasing financial problems on
every hand and the personal quarrels of the Oregon
mission, the Board, although they did not blame
Marcus and Narcissa in any way, felt that this drastic
step was the only possible solution.

This move was what Marcus had dreaded in his
harried waking moments and in his restless sleep. He
felt that Waiilatpu must be maintained because of
its strategic position on the pioneer trail, even if the
American Board sold it to another church group.
And, even more than this, he knew that the mission
was a center of strong Protestant activity in Oregon
—a center whose downfall would have a serious and

perhaps deadly effect on the growth of strong Protestant establishments in the Pacific Northwest.

Ironically enough, the fateful letter did not arrive in Oregon until September—several months after the quarreling missionaries had managed to reach a peaceful and amicable settlement of their problems.

In July, 1842, after the annual meeting of the Oregon mission, Marcus had written to Secretary Greene of the Board:

"We had a most plain talk with Mr. Spalding which resulted in his acknowledging himself to have been in the wrong in the leading causes of complaint and that he had been very jealous . . . he has pledged himself that he will not be so jealous and that he will cooperate with the Mission and most especially with Mrs. Whitman and myself. . . . We care little for these things so far as we are concerned as individuals but we feel deeply for any injury done to the Mission."

When the letter from the Board arrived at Waiilatpu, Marcus lost no valuable time in summoning all of the members of the mission together to discuss what must be done.

"I feel that someone must go back east immediately," he had told Narcissa when the letter arrived. "Someone must lay our situation clearly before the Board and see that a really fair arrangement is made.

We must not let this mission be destroyed because the Board doesn't have all the pertinent information. They are having a lot of financial trouble. They might decide to let the mission go even if they know that there is no longer any argument among us. Letters are so slow and so unsatisfactory that our work may be ended just as it is beginning to bear fruit."

"You are the one to go, Marcus," Narcissa said firmly. "It will be lonely here without you, but I know that you must go. You are the only one who can explain to the Board how much Waiilatpu means to the growth of the Christian faith in this far-off land."

"There are other reasons, too, why someone must return," Marcus continued. "It is not enough that the mission be kept alive. It must be kept growing and active. We have begun to make a few inroads. As this region grows, and it is bound to grow, it will be our great duty to see that Christianity is steadily strengthened. This means that every encouragement must be given to good Christian men to make the migration and to settle here among the Indians. What I would like to do is persuade the American Board to hire farmers and artisans to settle out here, or, at least, to encourage men of good character to do so. Do you know what I would like to see, Narcissa?" He turned away from her and went to the window, looking out at the fields and buildings of Waiilatpu. His mind traveled back to the few years ago when there had been nothing in this spot except, perhaps, wild horses grazing by the river. His eyes, usually so practical and resolute, filled with a great dream. And then, like the man of action that he was, he turned back toward his wife with a firm, determined step.

"I would like to see settled among all the Indian tribes a few men and women—Christians and workers—who could demonstrate by their daily lives the great advantages of civilized skills. Why, just a few people of that character could do more good in a year than we missionaries alone could do in ten!"

"It is a great dream you have, Marcus, and it is one that will come," Narcissa said gently, unwilling to disturb her husband's thoughts but unable to suppress the rising hopes which filled her heart. If he could talk this persuasively to the Board, there would never again be reason to fear that Waiilatpu would be destroyed.

"Perhaps, Narcissa," Marcus went on eagerly, only half hearing what she had said, "perhaps I could talk to people all the way back east. Encouragement is needed for good honest folk to come this far from their homes and relatives. Most of the pioneers we have had so far have been pretty rough. It is hard to convince them of the need for law and order."

"There was an attempt among the law-abiding citizens to set up a temporary government last year," Narcissa reminded him. "They didn't succeed, but they're going to try again this year."

"Yes, but the more good citizens we have here, the greater the chance that they can establish a government and show Congress that there is something here worthy of annexation. You know how I feel, Narcissa. The Oregon territory *must* become part of the United States. Anything we can do to bring more American citizens here will bring the goal that much closer."

"Won't there be considerable argument in the States over annexation?" argued Narcissa. "From what I've heard, the South would oppose it, because it would mean more free territory, and the slave states would be outnumbered in Congress."

"Oh, that would slow annexation down. But I've heard of a greater danger. The rumors are that Daniel Webster, the secretary of state, is about willing to give up the American claim to Oregon in exchange for a Newfoundland codfishery. He's a New Englander. He doesn't know how rich this country is and how much it would be worth to the United States."

Narcissa looked at her husband in wonder. "But,

Marcus, what could you do about that? He surely wouldn't even listen to you."

"Oh, that's true enough. But if there were hundreds of Americans living in the territory, it would be hard for the government to ignore them. Narcissa, if Americans come into this country, it's won, no matter what objections are raised in the East and the South." He struck one clenched fist into his open hand for emphasis.

"Do you think really large groups—large enough to do any good for Christian civilization in Oregon territory—could be persuaded to come here?" Narcissa said doubtfully, possible difficulties filling her mind. "You know it's more difficult than it was when we came to make the migration. The Indians are more suspicious than ever that the white men are trying to steal their land, and some of the good water holes have been poisoned or have dried up."

"Yes, they can be persuaded," Marcus answered confidently. "But first they must be convinced that wagons can come through. Otherwise, women and children will never come in large numbers. Without them, Oregon might better be left to the British for a private hunting ground. But wagons *can* come through. You remember that a few made the crossing back in 1840. If a number of wagons were banded together, the settlers could help each other, and it shouldn't be too difficult."

"The Hudson's Bay Company officials at Fort Hall will certainly warn parties that if they try to take wagons through, they'll all be caught by winter snows and starve to death. You know we have heard stories before about that."

"That's it, Narcissa. You've showed me one thing I can do. If a large party is gathered for next spring, I'll make it my business to see that I return with them. Somehow I'll manage to persuade them that they can come through on wheels."

"Wheels to Oregon! Oh, it would be wonderful! It would mean that there could be good solid citizens in this uncivilized country," Narcissa cried with excitement.

Marcus sighed. "Narcissa, you know my thoughts. You know that I believe that the Indians, to whom we came to bring the word of God, are slowly but surely dying out as tribes. We must do what we can to help them. But the future of this country lies with the white people. Our work from now on, if the whites come, is to see that good Christian settlements are made. This territory must be for Christ. That is our job. That must be the purpose of the rest of our lives."

13. RIDE TO THE EAST

THERE WAS NO LITTLE ARGUMENT among the other members of the Oregon mission when Marcus announced his plans to return to Boston to talk to the Board. Only too well did all of them know what would happen to the cause of Protestant Christianity in Oregon if the original orders of the Board should be carried out. And all of them quickly responded to Marcus' great vision of a mission expanded to render ever more valuable service to the Indians and to the new settlers.

But there were practical considerations, too, to be kept in mind, and sometimes Marcus Whitman was inclined to minimize practical considerations in his stubbornness—so some of his fellows thought.

"We can't spare you here for the months such a trip would take," insisted one missionary, "and you know very well that the Board would not approve because of the heavy expense. Why, I think that just a letter would be sufficient."

Marcus' face grew more determined. "Letters are of no good in this crisis. For years we have all been begging for more help in our work, but it is hard to put across in a letter the burning necessity for this help. Perhaps the Board will still turn us down, but it won't be for lack of information."

At last the matter was settled. Marcus was given the mission's approval to return east.

On October 3, 1842, in company with Mr. A. L. Lovejoy, who had come out the previous spring, Marcus set forth on the long and arduous journey to the Atlantic seaboard. He had only seven months to spend on his trip if he was to return in time to join the 1843 emigration to Oregon.

The two men knew that they would be traveling in winter, but they could not know that one of the worst winters known to the settlers was to descend upon them. At Fort Hall they were warned that the Indians were on the warpath. To avoid trouble, they were forced to take the much longer southern route, which cut days from Marcus' precious time. But this longer trail through what is now New Mexico probably saved their lives, for they missed the terrible mountain blizzards.

On the way to Taos from Fort Uncompagre, which

was situated on the Grand River (now recognized as part of the Colorado River), they were caught in a great snowstorm. Their guide looked about one morning and declared that the heavy snow had so changed the appearance of the country that he was completely lost.

After returning to Fort Uncompagre and hiring another and better guide, they managed to get on their way again. When they came once again to the banks of the Grand River, the guide decided that the current was too swift and the water too icy for them to cross safely.

Marcus, driven by his desperation and his limited time, mounted his horse and forced it into the water. The current was so swift that the animal could scarcely keep afloat or make any progress. Fighting inch by inch, thinking at each minute that he and the horse would be swept helplessly away, Marcus made his way across, landing a great distance downstream. Given courage by his success, Lovejoy and the guide crossed. The three men dried their frozen clothes and started again on their difficult journey.

At Bent's Fork, near present-day La Junta, Colorado, Marcus left Lovejoy. Traveling with a hunting party, he arrived in Westport, Kansas, in February. He had been traveling since October. Now, for the

first time, he was once more in a settled American
town.

Not a minute did he lose in preaching his Oregon
message. The great object of his journey lay in Boston, but he was no person to miss an opportunity to
awaken interest in the rich unsettled land of Oregon.
At every step on his long ride across the plains, he
talked. To church meetings, to dinner parties, to
people he met casually on the street, he talked of the
richness of the Oregon territory and of the need for
good Christian settlers in that distant land.

"Come," he said to all of them. "Come, and you
will find health and wealth and happiness. Bring
cattle and sheep. Bring wagons, but load them with
nothing but provisions that you will need on the journey. Come and help to save Oregon for Christ."

And people listened. Some listened because they
believed Oregon should be American. Some listened
because they believed that new free territory would
mean the end of slavery. Some listened because they
dreamed of wealth. But many listened because they
heard and understood Marcus' cry for "Christian settlement in Oregon."

Through snow and rain and sleet Marcus Whitman rode on into the east. He was a strange figure,
a modern Robinson Crusoe, as one person called him.
His hair long, his beard untrimmed, clothed in the

ragged buffalo coat and the buckskin breeches which he wore in the rough country of Oregon, he drew stares and jeers from strangers. But, uncouth as he was in appearance, there was an undying faith and courage in his face and voice that made the stranger stop to listen and to think.

In Washington he talked to James M. Porter, President Tyler's secretary of war. Marcus had gone to school with Porter, and he was able to reach him with little delay.

"Establish forts," he told the Secretary. "Establish forts along the emigrant trail into Oregon. These forts can raise supplies to help the travelers, so that they won't reach Oregon half-starved and naked. And they will provide protection against the Indians. It would be the greatest investment the United States could make in the future of the West."

"You are very convincing, Doctor," smiled Porter. "But you know well that I alone can't make this decision. You are in a hurry. Submit this plan to me in writing, and I will do everything I can to see that it gets attention. That's all I can promise you."

"That's all I can ask of you. I will do what you suggest." Marcus shook hands and left, joyful over even this small gain.

Once more he was on his way, still clad in rough buckskin and buffalo fur. On March 27, his time growing steadily shorter, he arrived in New York City. Without proper clothing, he soon found himself without money. Having lived too long among savages, he was an easy victim for a rascally cabman who fleeced him of most of his few remaining dollars. But this mishap did not deter him from his mission. He went directly to Horace Greeley, the famous editor of the great *New York Tribune.* If he could get the editorial support of this man, Marcus thought, he would have done more than if he stayed years in the East, talking steadily.

It was a disappointing visit. Horace Greeley's name was later to be linked forever with the famous command of "Go west, young man." But he was opposed, for political reasons, to the Oregon migration. A few months after Marcus' visit, speaking of the 1843 trek to Oregon, he called it the work of insane men.

The stubborn Marcus told him of the seven-foot wheat and the nine-foot corn and the fine herds of cattle, but Greeley was also a stubborn man who did not change his mind easily. It was small satisfaction he gave Marcus in his editorial the next day:

"We were most agreeably surprised yesterday by a call from Doctor Whitman from Oregon. . . . A slight glance at him when he entered our office would convince any one that he had seen all the hardships of a life in the wilderness. He was dressed in an old fur cap, that appeared to have seen some ten years' service, faded, and nearly destitute of fur; a vest whose natural color had long since faded, and a shirt —we could not see that he had any—an overcoat, every thread of which could be easily seen, buckskin pants. . . . The doctor is one of those daring and good men who went to Oregon some ten years ago to teach the Indians religion, agriculture, letters, etc. A noble pioneer we judge him to be, a man fitted to be chief in rearing a moral empire among the wild men of the wilderness. . . . He brings information that the settlers on the Willamette are doing well. . . ."

This was lukewarm enthusiasm indeed, and Marcus read it with a sinking heart. He was not interested in praise of himself, but support for Oregon.

But soon he was up and off again, to Boston, to face the American Board. It was a cold reception he found on Beacon Hill.

On receiving the letter from Whitman telling of the missionaries' peaceful settlement of their differences, the Board had written again ordering that the original letter be forgotten and the mission continued. This letter had, of course, been received in Oregon after the doctor had left. But, again, only nine days before his arrival in the Board's offices, another letter had been sent ordering him to obey their original orders. Now, instead of being in Oregon where he could carry out their directives, he was here, in Boston, standing before them in the most outlandish garb they had seen in many a year.

Marcus had known when he left Oregon that the Board would not be pleased by his visit, for no missionary was supposed to leave his post without permission. Furthermore, as he knew, the Board had little money, and none at all to spend on such unauthorized traveling.

But in spite of the Board's unfriendliness, the information he gave them saved the Oregon mission. His conviction of the importance of Waiilatpu was too strong and too appealing for him to be overruled. But the Board refused to give him everything he asked for.

Impressed though they were by his great plan of settling Christian farmers and artisans close to each Indian village, to teach useful skills, they felt that their small budget was already far too strained for them to shoulder the expense and, furthermore, that there was a definite question as to whether they could legally authorize funds for such a semi-missionary purpose.

And to his request that they make a positive and aggressive effort to encourage pastors and church members to remove to Oregon territory, they were cold. Such activity would be unsettling to the already established churches, and the Board could not take such a responsibility. If pastors and church members wished to go of their own accord, that was their business, but as for fostering such a plan—no, they could not do that.

However, Secretary Greene suggested, if Marcus himself wished to spend some time urging good Christian folk to transplant themselves to Oregon, they would have no objection. Just so long as it was made quite clear that the American Board would not be responsible in any way for their safety or financial care.

Disappointed but feeling that he had, after all, accomplished the most important purpose, the saving of Waiilatpu, Marcus Whitman turned westward again. With him this time was his nephew, Perrin Whitman, who was thirteen years old and greatly excited by the strange adventure before him.

Back to Westport, Kansas, they hurried, to join the great wagon train of the emigrants. Ahead of him, Marcus knew, lay one of the greatest battles of his life.

The wheels must go through to Oregon!

14. WHEELS TO OREGON

MARCUS WHITMAN RODE SLOWLY beside his nephew Perrin in the great cloud of dust. Ahead of them and behind them under the blazing sun stretched the long winding snake's tail of the wagon train.

"You're needed ahead, Doctor," cried a horseman as he rode up to them. "Mrs. Scott's baby is about to arrive."

Marcus spurred his horse to a gallop, Perrin following close behind.

At the Scotts' wagon, he dismounted and entered the wagon in what seemed a single leap. A few minutes of examination and he was out again.

"Don't look so scared, man," he told Jeff Scott, who stood by helplessly. "She's going to be all right. And, from the way it looks, it won't be long either. Pull your wagon out of the line as fast as you can and get a fire going."

Scott numbly obeyed.

Emigrants in other wagons watched curiously as the lone wagon pulled to the side of the trail. But they kept moving. There could be no delay. Again and again, when there was grumbling about the steady unending grind of travel, the doctor had told them: "You've got to keep moving. Travel. Travel. Make those twelve miles a day and you'll get to Oregon. Lose time, and you'll be in the Rocky Mountains at snow time."

A few hours later, the wagon train camped in its great circle. The guards were posted for the night; the cattle were turned loose to graze at will; the mules and horses milled in the great central space. Smoke from hundreds of campfires began to rise into the slowly darkening skies. The sound of a harmonica floated through the busy camp. Smells of coffee and frying bacon mingled with the odors of dust and sweat.

Suddenly the harmonica stopped. "Look," cried the player, "there comes Dr. Whitman. And look at the grin on Jeff's face. It must be a boy!"

The Scotts' wagon pulled up into the circle. Supper was forgotten as the women climbed eagerly into the wagon to see the new baby and to help the timid little Mrs. Scott. Men crowded around Jeff, shaking his hand and slapping him on the back in congratulation.

But Marcus had pulled away from the crowd with Perrin. Smiling, he watched the laughing men and the chattering women.

"You know, Perrin," he said, "as long as these people can get that excited about a newborn baby, you don't need to worry about whether they're going to be able to make this trip."

Perrin looked at him curiously. "You know you said when we left Westport that this would be an easy trip for you. There wouldn't be anybody depending on you the way there was when you came out first. Then you had to look after Aunt Narcissa and the Indian boys. It seems to me you've got about fifty times that many this time."

Marcus laughed. "A doctor always has people depending on him, I guess. One of the greatest things about being a doctor is that you can really help people."

He was silent a moment. Again he looked at the great circle of wagons. His face became serious.

"I've got a feeling, though, that the greatest help I can give these folks is coming a little later. It won't be a doctor's help. And before this trip is over, there will probably be plenty of them who won't like me very much for it, either."

There were almost a thousand people in the great wagon train which had left Westport about the middle of May. For easier traveling and camping, the caravan had divided into two main parts, and there were several smaller sections which had gone ahead. But all of them were close enough together that help could be given if there was trouble with the Indians or sickness. The second section of the train was the "cow column," which was commanded by Jesse Applegate. It was with him and Peter Burnett, another leader, that Marcus talked mostly about the problems and difficulties the caravan would face.

Many of the emigrants never saw Marcus, or even heard of him. But his talks with Applegate and Burnett, both of whom were to become important citizens of Oregon Territory and Oregon State, had much to do with deciding the fates of the hundreds of men who were bringing their wives and children, their cattle and sheep, to make a new life for themselves in the Far West.

Some of those who came had been influenced by Marcus himself on his trip to the East. Still others had seen his letters in the missionary papers. But most of them were rough, unsettled people, with no interest in establishing a Christian settlement in Oregon. They wanted nothing but a new opportunity to get ahead in life and to escape the poverty-stricken misery which had been all they had ever known.

There was rich land in Oregon, they had heard, and it was free. No landlords, no banks, no mortgages. There would be an even chance for everyone.

All of the emigrants, no matter what motives had put them on the weary trail, owed much to Marcus Whitman. Time and again during the journey, he showed them how to take their wagons across the swollen rivers by stretching green—not dried—buffalo hides around the frames and floating them across. Time and time again he swam rivers to take a towline to the opposite shore to help the wagons and carts across. On one occasion, at least, he swam back and forth across a river for three days before he could find a passable ford. He won the confidence and the gratitude of the leaders of the caravan. Others might complain that he was a busybody and a meddler, but the leaders knew that he had found a way when no one else could.

As they approached Fort Hall, his hopes that they would take his last great piece of advice and encouragement rose. If they did not, many would die. Many would lose their cattle. Many would turn back to Kansas, and the cause of Oregon as a stronghold of Protestantism and a territory of the United States would be set back at least a year, perhaps forever.

When they reached the fort, he rode ahead to search out the best trail for the wagons. As he returned, his mind busy with plans for handling the wagons through the terrible country of the high sage grass that stretched westward from Fort Hall into the great barrier of the Blue Mountains, Perrin ran up to him.

"What is it, boy?" exclaimed Marcus, looking at his excited, worried face, and trying to understand what he was saying. "Here, slow down. I can't make out a word."

Perrin swallowed hard. "Captain Grant of the Hudson's Bay Company has been talking to Mr. Burnett and Mr. Applegate and some of the other emigrants. He's told them that they can't hope to take their wagons through. Some of the emigrants are talking about turning back, because they don't think they'll be able to get enough horses to carry them."

Marcus straightened up. His mouth became a grim line. This was the crisis he had been waiting for.

Quickly he searched through the fort for the caravan's leaders. On every side, women sat weeping, complaining that now everything would be lost. A few men whom he had persuaded to take the journey looked at him angrily. Some even stopped him and asked if they had come this far to be cheated by his foolish promises.

To all of them he replied that wagons could go through. "Don't worry. Let me talk to Mr. Burnett and Mr. Applegate. We'll figure out some way. Above all, don't think of turning back."

Finally he found the leaders, drinking coffee from their tin mugs. They were silent, their faces creased with worry and fatigue.

"Hello, Dr. Whitman," Jesse Applegate hailed him. "You find a discouraged company. Half of the emigrants are ready to leave and are blaming us and you for having led them after a will-o'-the-wisp."

"So I've just heard. Judging from the dark looks I got in the fort, my advice is none too popular."

"What do you say now, Doctor?" asked Jeff Scott. "I, for one, will do whatever you advise. I remember well how you helped my wife on the trail."

Marcus smiled gratefully at him. "That gives me the courage to speak out," he told Jeff. He turned to the rest of the men around the fire. Men and women and children were slowly crowding around; their angry and disappointed voices quieted. Only the shuffling of feet and the stamping and low brays of the grazing mules could be heard. Every eye was fixed anxiously on the buckskin-clad doctor, the Oregon veteran.

"Men and women of the train," Marcus began quietly, "you have heard from Captain Grant that beyond here there is no trail for wagons. I tell you that there is. In 1840, wagons were brought through. They stopped at my mission station in the Place of Rye Grass, which is beyond the Blue Mountains. I won't try to fool you. They weren't in very good condition. It was, and still is, a hard road for wagons. But they had come through.

"Captain Grant tells you that you can't take cattle through. I, for one, took cattle through in 1836. They were footsore and pretty thin, but they got through. Those cattle became a fine herd.

"Captain Grant has told you that you will all be caught by the great western blizzards and die. I tell you that you will reach the Columbia Valley before the snow, but that you must keep moving.

"I tell you that after you have crossed the Blue Mountains you will be able to take your wagons and your supplies and your cattle on rafts and boats down the Columbia River into the Willamette Valley.

"And in the valley you will find the richest land in all the continent of North America. Oregon doesn't yet belong completely to the United States. It never will unless you are willing to endure the labor and hardship to take your wagons and your cattle and your families across the Blue Mountains."

He stopped and looked at the intent faces about him. "How many of you are willing to go on to en-

sure that someday the boundaries of the United
States of America will stretch from the Atlantic to
the Pacific? How many of you are willing to stake
your future to determine that someday the flag of
the United States and the banner of God will rule
the territory of Oregon?"

A man cheered. In a moment, the doctor was surrounded by men and women, clasping his hand, slapping him on the back, and shouting for Marcus Whitman and the United States of America.

"Doctor, you are a wonder," said Jesse Applegate
a little later, when the noise had quieted and the
emigrants had gone cheerfully back to their work of
repairing wagons and reloading supplies. "I thought
surely you'd never convince those folks."

"God gave me words, Mr. Applegate. It is he whom
you must thank. And it is he who will see us through.
It is going to be very hard."

It was. Marcus, with Perrin and several others
from the train, went ahead to blaze a trail. But many
times they had to return to the train to help the great
unwieldy wagons over the rough ground and through
the high grass. Some of them were torn to pieces,
axles were broken, wheels were lost—but most of them
kept on the trail.

Many a time the men cursed the doctor and the

fool's errand he had led them on, but they kept on. Each nightfall found them a little closer to their goal.

In the Grande Ronde Valley, on the east side of the Blue Mountains, Marcus Whitman was met by one of his good Indian friends and converts, who was to be true to the very end. This was Chief Istickus. He brought a message from the Spaldings urging Marcus to hurry on to their Lapwai mission among the Nez Percés as soon as possible. There was serious illness.

"The train is all right now," Marcus told Peter Burnett. "There is rough going ahead through the Blue Mountains, but Chief Istickus will stay with you as a guide. You must be sure, too, not to try the short cut to the Dalles of the Columbia by the Malheur River. It is a very dangerous route—really impassable, I think. So don't be tempted by its apparent shortness."

Marcus' warning was to be forcefully brought home two years later when a party chose the Malheur River trail and was almost destroyed.

As Marcus prepared to leave immediately by horseback—the transportation he had used all the weary miles from the East—Peter Burnett and Jesse Applegate came to say good-by.

"Doctor, we want you to know that without you we would probably have never come this far. We wouldn't have had the courage or the determination," said Burnett simply.

Marcus smiled as he shook hands with them. "If I have done anything to help the wagons into Oregon, I will feel that I have given both to God and to my country the greatest service I could. If I never do another thing, I shall be satisfied."

As Marcus and Perrin Whitman rode hastily on into the west toward Lapwai, the great caravan got underway. The weary, patient oxen strained at the heavy wagons as the drivers shouted encouragingly at the animals and cracked their whips sharply over their heads. A few slow families hurriedly broke up their fires and piled into their wagons and onto their horses. Slowly, the long train began to move.

The wheels were on the trail to Oregon.

15. AMERICAN TERRITORY

AFTER ONE NIGHT AT LAPWAI, where he found the Spaldings recovered from scarlet fever, Marcus rode the ninety miles to Waiilatpu.

Narcissa had not spent the winter at the station because of ill health. Although she might have insisted on trying to recover without the aid of doctors, an unfriendly night intruder who tried to force his way into her room had made her staying alone for very long impossible. With the two little girls whom she was rearing at their fathers' request—Helen Mar, the daughter of Joseph Meek, one of the mountain men, and Mary Ann, the daughter of Jim Bridger, whose name will be famous as long as history books are written—she had gone to Fort Walla Walla. After a visit there, she had journeyed on to the Methodist station in the Willamette Valley, and the remainder of the long winter she had spent in the relative comfort of Fort Vancouver, where she could receive good medical care and relax in the town's congenial company.

But during her absence, Marcus found, the Place of Rye Grass had fallen prey to neglect and destruction. The Indians had burned the precious gristmill during his absence—a loss which would work great hardship upon Indians and whites alike when it was time to grind the wheat and corn. Troubling thoughts of the future overwhelmed Marcus as he gazed upon the shambles, for the vandalism meant that there was anger among the Indians. There was sure to be more trouble.

He found, too, that outriders of the emigrant train had reached the station, broken into the house, and willfully destroyed property.

"Ah, well," he sighed to himself as he turned away to start the two-hundred-mile ride to another mission station, again on a mission of mercy, "it takes all kinds to open a new country."

By the time he was able to return to Waiilatpu, many wagons had passed by the station. Their supplies gone, the hungry settlers had taken wheat and corn and vegetables from the Waiilatpu fields. But they had not been vandals, and they had known that they were welcome.

To speed his work of helping the travelers, Marcus

rigged a temporary wheel to grind his wheat and corn. Day after day he supplied the wagon train with food, with clothing, with fresh horses, and with helpers. Finally, the last stragglers from the train passed down the valley, and Marcus found that there was little food left. There was not even enough for his own family or for the exploring party of John Frémont, the great Pathfinder, which had followed the train across the plains and mountains.

"It will be almost like starting again," Marcus told Narcissa ruefully as he brought her back to Waiilatpu. "We do have a few potatoes, though. But next year we must raise much more so that we won't run short."

In the years that followed, Waiilatpu supplied many a family with food and shelter. The starving and the sick and the naked and the orphaned were never turned away from its doors.

Narcissa's health improved after the spring of 1844, and she willingly took in the many families who crowded her threshold during the fall of each year seeking help or care and medicine.

One afternoon she came out of the house to greet a wagon which had pulled up in front of the mission. She could see that there were several little children peeping out at her, and she could hear the wails of an infant.

"I've got your children here, Mrs. Whitman!" shouted the driver.

"My children!" she exclaimed in surprise. "Why, my children are all here at home."

The man laughed. "No, Mrs. Whitman, I don't mean them. These children that I have here are orphans, seven of them. Their mother and father died on the trail. The youngest is a tiny baby. Before their mother died, she said that I was to bring them to you. She had heard that you were an angel."

"But, seven children—" hesitated Narcissa.

An old woman walked up to her and laid the tiny baby in her arms.

"Why, this baby doesn't look more than a month old."

"She's five months," replied the driver.

"Why, the poor little thing must have been starved. Look how sickly and thin and pale she is. We must go right in and see that she has a warm bath and some warm milk."

Then and there Narcissa decided inside her heart that she would welcome these homeless children to her family. Their name was Sager, and although she and Marcus adopted them, they encouraged the children to keep their family name in memory of their father and mother, who had lost their lives on the Oregon trail.

Narcissa already had six children to care for, the children of hunters and settlers and Indians, whom she was rearing as her own. Never could her heart feel empty of love and care, although she sometimes yet longed for her own little Alice. But she was mother now to a larger family than she had ever dreamed of.

There was work for all. As soon as a child was old enough, he was given a definite chore which he was expected to perform, and each of them became proud of his ability to do his own work without prompting or scolding. But life at Waiilatpu was not all work.

There was fun for all of them, too. One of their greatest pleasures was a daily cold bath. Each day, winter and summer alike, the boys and girls took a quick plunge into the Walla Walla River. This was against all medical teachings, for people in those days thought that even night air carried all kinds of terrible diseases.

The years passed quickly. There were the usual petty troubles and quarrels with the Indians, but Narcissa and Marcus felt that their tireless work was at last bearing fruit, for many of the Indians seemed to understand the teachings of the Bible, and they came eagerly to the Sunday services and sent their children to the school to learn to read and write.

The successful emigration of 1843 had determined

that Oregon would fall to the United States. More than a thousand people entered in that year, and each year after that saw ever greater numbers pouring into the empty land. At last, neat farms dotted the vast Willamette Valley, and smoke from friendly chimneys filled skies that had known nothing but an occasional Indian campfire.

But there was still lacking the formality of a decisive treaty between the United States and Great Britain. On June 15, 1846, this treaty was concluded, although it was several months before the news arrived in Oregon. The 49th parallel was set as the boundary between Canada and the United States, and the mighty land of Oregon became American territory.

Now the settlers who had staked their property and their lives on Oregon could plan for the future, because once more law would govern their affairs.

"To be in a country among a people of no law, even if they are from a civilized land, is the nearest like a hell on earth of anything I can imagine," Narcissa had once written to her family.

The absence of law meant that settlers could not legally claim land they settled on, but that they could easily, by their very absence, lose property which they had in the States. They could not sign mortgages. They could not be sure that their wills would be carried out after their deaths. Their cattle fell to wolves, and no bounty could be established for killing the animals.

Now, at last, with ownership by the United States established, a sane and secure order could be brought again into their lives.

The government at Washington was to be slow to establish a territorial government in Oregon. It was to take war and massacre to speed Congress to action, but the mere prospect of federal control encouraged the settlers to plan for a hopeful future and to sink deep roots into the Oregon soil.

The treaty meant, too, that the territory governed by the United States stretched from the Atlantic to the Pacific. Only California remained ouside the fold on the Pacific coast; and soon it, too, by treaty with Spain, was to become American land. And it was to be not much longer before the discovery of gold at Sutter's mill in fabled California was to bring more Americans to the Far West than had ever been drawn by the riches of the Oregon land.

Among the Indian lodges, fears were aroused by the growing American migration into Oregon. The hated white man was now, indeed, pouring into the last hunting grounds of the red man by the hundreds and the thousands. Soon there would be little land left for the Indian. His buffalo would be killed off.

His rivers would be fished out. His streams and water holes would be polluted and destroyed. And he would die.

Some of the Indians, knowing that this would come to pass, tried to make peace with the white man and learn his ways. They took eagerly to learning the arts of farming and irrigation and cattle raising. They built fences, like him, around land that had been open and free for as long as their tribal memories went back. They took to the white man's God with eagerness and piety.

But there were others who preferred to make a fight for their homeland. Although the stories which had come out of the east about other tribes taught them that they could not win against the white man's superior numbers and weapons, they felt it was better to die than to be dishonored by abandoning their tribal traditions and pitifully copying the white man's ways.

Marcus and Narcissa knew of the heavy sorrow and anger troubling the spirits of the Indians, and they felt deeply for their red brothers, whom they had taught and worked beside. But they knew, too, that the future of Oregon lay now with the white man. To them the greatest service they could offer was to teach the Indian to bear his trouble with

patience and to accept the new ways with cheer-
fulness.

If there were a serious outbreak before the strength
of the white settlers became established in Oregon,
only death and destruction, fire and pillage, could be
their lot.

It was up to them, Marcus and Narcissa, to be a
calming barrier between the growing fury of the
Indians and the helpless white people. The Indians
would lose eventually; they would be severely punished by the United States. But needless and in-
nocent lives would be lost in the terrible upheaval
of a desperate last stand.

16. MASSACRE!

IT WAS LATE FALL in the year 1847. Waiilatpu was crowded. Eight pioneer families had decided to spend the winter at the Place of Rye Grass and there were, as well, the Whitmans' large family of children and several children from the other missions who were attending the school.

An epidemic of measles was raging through the Indian village, and it had struck, too, in the mission settlement.

John Sager, the eldest of the orphans taken in by Narcissa, and his sister Catherine were just recovering from the disease. Little Louise Sager and Helen Mar Meek lay in delirium, and several of the new settlers were bedridden and helpless.

There had been many deaths among the Indians. Marcus had visited most of them and given them medicine and good nursing, but they had insisted on following their tribal treatment and had ignored his good advice. They would steam themselves in their sweathouses, and then run, dripping with perspiration, to plunge into the icy river. Effective as this treatment was with a cold, it spelled death with measles.

On Marcus Whitman was placed the blame. He had put an evil spell upon them and given them poison, his Cayuse enemies whispered. From lodge to lodge the rumor spread.

Late one night when the epidemic was at its worst, Marcus returned from a mercy trip to a distant Cayuse village. He had gone with Henry Spalding, who had visited Waiilatpu to leave his daughter Eliza at the school. Mr. Spalding had lingered at the village, planning a more leisurely return, but Marcus had rushed back, his heart full of dread for his family and his guests.

He had visited with Istickus, the friendly Cayuse who had guided the great wagon train of 1843 from Fort Boise.

Istickus, in his grave way, had warned him, "You must leave this country. There is talk that you are to be killed."

As calmly as he could, Marcus replied, "I will never leave unless God wills it. I have offered many times before to leave if the Indians do not want me, and each time they ask me to stay."

Istickus insisted, "You must go. My people have bad hearts. They are made angry by the many white men who have come here. They will kill you."

Marcus arrived home about midnight, exhausted by his long hours in the saddle and by his fear, not for himself but for the helpless families at the mission. He found Narcissa asleep in the parlor, for all the bedrooms had been given up to the sick or to the newly arrived families.

She awoke immediately and started up as she saw the deep worry in his face, although he tried to smile.

"What has happened, Marcus? You were concerned about the sickness and the trouble with the Indians when you left last evening, but something more has happened."

"Yes," he sighed, passing his hand over his eyes. "I saw Istickus and he warned me to leave. He warned me against Joe Lewis, the Canadian half-breed. He said Lewis has been urging the Cayuse to kill me because I am a bad *te-wat*."

"We have done a great deal for Joe Lewis since he arrived here with no food and clothing," the usually calm Narcissa said with anger. "But he has always hated us. Other Indians have cautioned us against him."

"I have tried to send him away, but he won't go," replied Marcus wearily.

He sat down heavily by the stove and bowed his grizzled head upon his work-worn calloused hands. After a moment of silence he looked up at his troubled wife, who was looking around the room at the sick children who lay sleeping there.

"Narcissa," he said quietly, "You know that the Cayuse are using the deaths of my patients merely as an excuse. They are really angry because we have helped and protected the white settlers. They are angry because we have tried to teach a new religion and to destroy the old tribal pagan beliefs."

Narcissa's mouth was trembling, but she managed to smile a little.

"I know that, Marcus. They will want to kill both of us and the white settlers who are here at Waii-latpu."

"Are you afraid, my dear?" he asked.

"Of course I am," his wife replied. "I would be lying if I said I were not. But if we must die now, we shall die together. And we shall die knowing that we have given our lives for our faith in God."

"You give me great courage to face the morning,

Narcissa," Marcus said gratefully, taking her hands
in his own and pressing them affectionately.

Narcissa struggled to regain her composure and
to consider their danger without unreasoning panic.
"Perhaps we are making too much of this, dear.
Perhaps this trouble will be no worse than the time
Tilaukait struck you and ordered you to leave."

"I hear that Tilaukait is among those who are
talking against me this time," answered Marcus. "He
says that the white man has come to destroy the
Indian, but that the Indian will destroy him first.
Perhaps it is idle boasting, but I want to see that
the children, at least, are moved to Fort Walla Walla
as soon as they can travel. Now go to bed, Narcissa.
You will need all the rest you can get. I will sit up
with the sick children."

Narcissa went to bed. Throughout the few remaining hours of the night, she woke again and again to
see her husband sitting by the flickering light of the
stove, his head bowed in prayer.

The morning of November 29 dawned foggy. Soon
the bustle of a Monday morning at the mission took
Marcus' mind from his worries. He felt that the fears
of the night before had been due to his weariness.
In the light of morning everything looked brighter.
Even the trouble in Narcissa's face faded as she
listened to his cheerful voice giving the orders for

the day. A steer was to be slaughtered for the weekly
meat, and grain was to be loaded on ponies and sent
off to the Lapwai mission. A short distance from the
mission house the blacksmith's anvil rang and a
hammer pounded at the laying of a new floor.

Narcissa walked out into the yard for a breath of
air when the household chores were well started.
There were certainly lots of Indians about, she
noticed idly, and they didn't seem to be doing much
of anything. Only a few of them had come to the
funeral of a dead Indian child which Marcus had
conducted that morning, but she had thought they
were simply afraid of catching the disease.

For a moment, fear for her children and the helpless families filled her mind again, but she resolutely
shook it off. No, she wouldn't borrow trouble. Marcus
had enough on his mind without bothering him with
a trifle. She went back into the house and busied
herself by bathing the children, while her husband
worked on his account books, looking up with a smile
at the splashings and laughter.

Suddenly, in the midst of the gay scene, there was
a knock at the door between the sitting room and
the kitchen. Mary Ann Bridger, who was washing
dishes in the kitchen, called to Marcus that Chief
Tilaukait and his friend Tomahas wanted to see him.

Narcissa looked anxiously at Marcus. He smiled

and shrugged his shoulders. "I guess they want to tell me again that I am a bad man and an evil *te-wat*. Don't worry, dear."

He entered the kitchen and closed the door.

"Good afternoon, Tilaukait," he said courteously as he sat down by the fire.

"I come again to tell you—" Tilaukait began.

Suddenly Marcus received a terrific blow on his head. A second blow knocked him to the floor unconscious. Tomahas, who came to be called "the Murderer," had stepped behind the doctor and struck him with a clay tomahawk. John Sager, who was making brooms in the kitchen, was shot to death.

The Indians fled.

Mary Ann rushed through the kitchen door to the yard, and around the house to the sitting room. Hysterically she told the unbelieving and stunned Narcissa what had happened. The frightened children, half-dressed and screaming, began to flee from the house.

Calmly and sternly, her face a white mask, Narcissa called them back.

Through the open door rushed one of the settlers, his arm shattered by a musket ball. "They're killing us all!" he shouted in terror.

Still calm, Narcissa helped him to a chair and brought him water. Then she closed and locked the doors to the house and pulled her husband, who was still alive, into the sitting room.

Outside there were bursts of gunfire and the screams and shouts of wounded men. At the sound of the shot which had killed John Sager, the Indians had opened fire on the men working outside the house. Most of them were killed, but one escaped to carry a warning to Lapwai. All of them realized that this was but the start of a full-scale Indian uprising. The mission at Waiilatpu had simply been chosen as the first white settlement to fall.

Andrew Rodgers, a young man who was serving as an assistant to the missionaries and who was studying for the ministry, had been in the garden when the first shot—the one that killed John Sager— was fired. He hid until he saw a good chance to reach the house and then ran for the sitting room door. Wounded in the arm, he struck the sash-door to the living room with such force that he shattered the glass. Quickly Narcissa unlocked the door to let him in. In that moment, as she stood exposed, a musket was fired and Narcissa fell, wounded, crying, "Lord, save these little ones."

But she did not lose her presence of mind. She knew that there was no hope for her life, for she would be among the first they would want to kill.

But the children, surely they would not harm the children, she prayed.

Gasping as she spoke, she ordered that everybody go upstairs. There, unless the Indians decided to burn the house with everybody in it, they would have more protection.

Soon, the Indians, now jubilant with their easy victory, entered the downstairs, breaking down doors and smashing windows. In the sitting room they found the living but unconscious doctor and cruelly slashed his face with their knives. John Sager's body they mutilated horribly.

At last the Indians offered truce, and an agreement was reached by Narcissa and Tomahas, who suggested that the party go to another building in the mission. There was nothing to be gained by refusing.

"Bring the children's clothing," Narcissa ordered, "and whatever else you can carry that you will need. They will surely burn the house now."

She was still strangely calm, still turning her mind to means to pacify the Indians.

Not until she passed through the sitting room and saw her husband's mutilated face did she lose her composure. She stumbled and nearly fainted. Quickly, Andrew Rodgers, who had been like a brother to her, caught her as she fell and laid her on a settee.

"We had better carry her on the settee," he said to Joe Lewis, the half-breed who had talked against the Whitmans. "She'll never make it if she walks." Francis Sager was stationed by the Indians at the head of the column. Through the north door of the kitchen the little group passed. Outside the door stood a semicircle of Indians, armed with muskets. Lewis dropped the front end of the settee and ran. Quick musket-fire enveloped Francis Sager and Narcissa and Andrew Rodgers.

Narcissa slipped from the settee and fell to the wet ground, her body pierced by two bullets.

Narcissa and Marcus Whitman were dead, heroes of Oregon, martyrs to Christ.

17. MARTYRS OF OREGON

WHEN THE TERRIBLE MASSACRE was over, thirteen people had been killed by the Indians. Little Helen Mar Meek and Louise Sager died during their captivity of illness and lack of care. Over forty white people, mostly children, were held for ransom. Several escaped. The buildings of the mission were burned.

Henry Spalding, hearing of the tragedy from a friendly Indian on his way to Waiilatpu, escaped to Lapwai riding by night and hiding by day. He found that the Nez Percés had refused to join the Cayuse on the warpath and were protecting his family.

It was yet another month before the captives could be ransomed from the Indians with blankets, guns, tobacco, and food, largely contributed by the Hudson's Bay Company.

With Indian permission, the bodies of the dead had been buried by the survivors soon after the massacre. But there was no rest yet for the victims.

When Joseph Meek, the father of little Helen Mar and an important man in Oregon, passed through Waiilatpu on his way to Washington to report on the horror and to carry a petition asking for a territorial government, he found that wolves had torn open the graves and that the bones of the dead lay scattered around the clearing. Gathering them up, he gently placed them in a common grave beneath a mound of dirt.

President James K. Polk quickly saw to it that action was taken on Oregon by Congress. After an all-night session, a territorial government for Oregon was established and Joseph Meek was appointed to the post of United States marshal.

The Christian law and civilization that Marcus and Narcissa Whitman had dreamed of were at last to be established in the dark land of Oregon. They did not see the fulfillment of their dreams and hopes and tireless work, but in the hearts of the white settlers they were enshrined forever as those who, with the help of God, had brought it to pass.

EPILOGUE

IN THE GREAT RELIGIOUS REVIVAL which swept the United States at the end of the eighteenth century, a group of dedicated men became convinced that it was not always enough for a Christian to strive to make his own life as Christlike as possible. In distant lands there were thousands of people who had never heard of the teachings of Christ. Out of the conviction that Christianity should be brought to these peoples grew the American Board of Commissioners for Foreign Missions.

Since the first small band of missionaries sailed from the friendly shores of New England to far Calcutta, India, in February, 1812, thousands of names, most of them unsung and forgotten, have been added to the annals of the missionary society. Many of those who pledged themselves to the service of Christ in foreign lands died the deaths of the martyred, but the danger of the work seemed to serve as a challenge, rather than as a barrier, for the roll of names continued to grow. Today, the news reports are filled with terrible stories of the persecution which is being visited upon the missionaries, for example, in China. But today, as always, there is a great need for more and more young men and women in the work of the foreign missions.

It is against this background of devotion and self-sacrifice that Marcus and Narcissa Whitman take their proper place in history, for in their eyes, as in the eyes of their fellow missionaries, they were not going beyond the call of duty in risking their lives.

To Americans the Whitmans stand as symbols of the far-reaching missionary work and of the undaunted pioneer spirit that led to the settlement of the wild, untraveled American West. For these services, they have been honored many times.

Perhaps the greatest monument to Marcus Whitman's courage and vision is Whitman College, in Walla Walla, Washington, only a few miles from the site of Waiilatpu. Dr. Whitman often spoke of the need for a Christian college in the Oregon territory, and in 1859, under the auspices of the Congregational Churches, the institution was founded by the Reverend Cushing Eels, one of the first workers in the Oregon mission.

In 1897, the fiftieth anniversary of the massacre, a great monument was erected on a hill near the mission site in honor of the victims, and a few months later their bodies were disinterred and reburied in their final resting place beneath a great marble slab, on which their names were engraved.

In 1936, the Whitman Centennial Celebration Corporation succeeded in having passed by Congress a bill creating the Whitman National Monument. Money was raised by the corporation to buy forty-five acres of the site of the original mission, and archaeologists of the National Park Service, which has charge of all national monuments, set to work to determine the exact plan of the mission as it had been before its destruction. Today, the sites of the original buildings have been located and marked. The Monument, which is open daily, is six miles west of Walla Walla and may be easily reached by the interested visitor.

In recognition of Dr. Whitman's services to the cause of Oregon, he was selected by the state of Washington as a state hero, and in the spring of 1953 his statue was placed in Statuary Hall in the Capitol Building in Washington, D.C.

These are great honors indeed, but they are only a few of the memorials to the Whitmans' great service to the spread of Christianity and to their country. For a full listing, the interested reader is referred to Dr. Clifford M. Drury's *Marcus Whitman, M.D.* (Caxton Printers, 1937).

ABOUT THE AUTHOR

ANN WEST WILLIAMS has had long experience as an editor and a literary agent, and, in collaboration with her husband, as a researcher in religious history. She won a Phi Beta Kappa key at the University of North Carolina, and received a Master's Degree in American Literature at the University of Denver. Although this is her first book for teen-age readers, she has been co-editor of the HEROES OF GOD project from its inception. She is active in the Episcopal Church in Littleton, Colorado, her home.